MONOCULTURE

*How One Story is
Changing Everything*

F.S. Michaels

**RED
CLOVER**
redcloverpress.com

For my friends and family, who helped me stay the course.

Grateful acknowledgement is made to the following: Princeton University Press for permission to quote selections from *Available Light*, by Clifford Geertz. Copyright © 2000 by Clifford Geertz. Smithsonian Institution Scholarly Press for permission to quote selections from *Beauty and the Beasts: On Museums, Art, the Law, and the Market*, by Stephen Weil. Copyright © 1983 by Stephen Weil. Springer Science+Business Media for permission to quote selections from "Academic work satisfaction in the wake of institutional reforms in Australia," 2005, Craig McInnis and Malcolm Anderson, in *The Professoriate*, edited by Anthony Welch. Copyright © 2005. PuddleDancer Press for permission to quote selections from *Nonviolent Communication: A Language of Life*, by Dr. Marshall B. Rosenberg. Copyright © 2003 by Marshall B. Rosenberg.

LIBRARY AND ARCHIVES CANADA CATALOGUING IN PUBLICATION
Michaels, F. S.
    Monoculture : how one story is changing everything / by FS Michaels.
Includes bibliographical references and index.
Also issued in electronic format.
ISBN 978-0-9868538-0-7
    1. Economics--Sociological aspects. 2. Culture--Economic aspects.
    3. Civilization--21st century. I. Title.
HM548.M53 2011   306.3   C2011-901323-1

Published in Canada in 2011 by Red Clover Press
www.redcloverpress.com
Printed in the United States of America
15 14 13 12 11   1 2 3 4 5

MONOCULTURE

CONTENTS

It is easy to forget how mysterious and mighty stories are. They do their work in silence, invisibly. They work with all the internal materials of the mind and self. They become part of you while changing you. Beware the stories you read or tell; subtly, at night, beneath the waters of consciousness, they are altering your world.

—BEN OKRI

1

WHAT IS A MONOCULTURE?

There is no such thing as just a story. A story is always charged with meaning...And we can be sure that if we know a story well enough to tell it, it carries meaning for us.

—ROBERT FULFORD

THE HISTORY OF HOW we think and act, said twentieth-century philosopher Isaiah Berlin, is, for the most part, a history of dominant ideas. Some subject rises to the top of our awareness, grabs hold of our imagination for a generation or two, and shapes our entire lives. If you look at any civilization, Berlin said, you will find a particular pattern of life that shows up again and again, that rules the age. Because of that pattern, certain ideas become popular and others fall out of favor. If you can isolate the governing pattern that a culture obeys, he believed, you can explain and understand the world that shapes how people think, feel and act at a distinct time in history.[1]

The governing pattern that a culture obeys is a master story — one narrative in society that takes over the others, shrinking diversity and forming a monoculture. When you're inside a master story at a particular time in history, you tend to accept its definition of reality. You unconsciously believe and act on certain things, and disbelieve and fail to act on other things. That's the power of the monoculture; it's able to direct us without us knowing too much about it.

Over time, the monoculture evolves into a nearly invisible foundation that structures and shapes our lives, giving us our sense of how the world works. It shapes our ideas about what's normal and what we can expect from life. It channels our lives in a certain direction, setting out strict boundaries that we unconsciously learn to live inside. It teaches us to fear and distrust other stories; other stories challenge the monoculture simply by existing, by representing alternate possibilities.

As a result, learning to see the monoculture can leave us feeling threatened and anxious because the process exposes our foundations, outlines the "why" of why we live the way we do. Still, if we fail to understand how the monoculture shapes our lives and our world, we're at risk of making decisions day after day without ever really understanding how our choices are being predetermined, without understanding how the monoculture even shapes what we think our options are. Without a clear understanding of the monoculture, it's hard to understand the trajectory of your own life. But once you know what shared beliefs and assumptions make up the governing pattern at this point in history, you can discover the consequences of the monoculture and decide if that's how you really want to live.

Monocultures and their master stories rise and fall with the times. By the seventeenth century, for example, the master story revolved around science, machines and mathematics. Developments in fields like biology, anatomy, physics, chemistry and astronomy were early harbingers of modern science. People began to believe that the nature of the world could be discovered through mathematics, that physical laws directed the behavior of all bodies, and that living creatures could be systematically catalogued in relation to one another. Life was understood as a series of questions with knowable answers, and the world became methodical and precise. A scientific monoculture was created.

That scientific monoculture was radically different from the religious monoculture that preceded it. If you had lived in sixteenth century Europe, a hundred years earlier, you would almost certainly have understood your life through the master story of religion and superstition. People lived surrounded by angels and demons. When Galileo contradicted the teachings of the Roman Catholic Church by claiming that the sun and not the Earth was at the center of the solar system, he was accused of heresy and sentenced to house arrest for the rest of his life. Excommunication from the church and the damning of your eternal soul was a real threat, and you could literally pay for your sins to guarantee yourself a short stay in purgatory. Religion was the zeitgeist, the spirit of the age.

A monoculture doesn't mean that everyone believes exactly the same thing or acts in exactly the same way, but that we end up sharing key beliefs and assumptions that direct our lives. Because a monoculture is mostly left unarticulated until it has been displaced years later, we learn its boundaries by trial and error. We somehow come to know how the master story goes, though no one tells us exactly what the story is or what its rules are. We develop a strong sense of what's expected of us at work, and in our families and communities — even if we sometimes choose not to meet those expectations. We usually don't ask ourselves where those expectations came from in the first place. They just exist — or they do until we find ourselves wishing things were different somehow, though we can't say exactly what we would change, or how.

Monocultures, though overwhelmingly persuasive and pervasive, aren't inescapable. In the end, the human experience always diverges from the monoculture and its master story, because our humanity is never as one-dimensional as the master story says it is. The human experience is always wider and deeper than a single narrative, and over time, we become hungry for something the monoculture isn't speaking to and isn't giving us — can't give us. Once you know what the monoculture looks like, you can decide whether it serves a useful purpose in your life, or whether you want to transcend it and live in a wider spectrum of human values instead — to know it so you can leave it behind.

In our time, in the early decades of the twenty-first century, the monoculture isn't about science, machines and mathematics, or about religion and superstition. In our time, the monoculture is economic. Because of the rise of the economic story, six areas of your world are changing — or have already changed — in subtle and not-so-subtle ways. How you think about your work, your relationships with others and the natural world, your community, your physical and spiritual health, your education, and your creativity are being shaped by economic values and assumptions.

And because how you think shapes how you act, the monoculture that arises as a result isn't just changing your mind — it's changing your life.

2

THE ONE STORY

Generally, the familiar, precisely because it is familiar, is not known.

—Hegel

"The universe," said poet Muriel Rukeyser, "is made of stories, not of atoms." Stories are what we are made of too. We use them to capture our yesterdays and secure our tomorrows. Stories tell us what we can expect from other people, and from life. There are as many ways to tell them as there are people in the world, and as many stories waiting to be told. Those that resonate deeply stay with us all our lives. A good story, well told, makes you realize you were yearning for something you had no name for, something you didn't even know you wanted.

In one sense, we are constantly telling stories. We live them every day, playing everything from minor to major roles in other people's lives. Somehow we take all of these different narratives we're part of and weave them into something that helps us understand why things are the way they are. As storytellers, we make sense of our lives through our own point of view, giving meaning to one thing or another according to how we each make sense of the world. How do we do it? How do we make sense of where we come from and where we are going? What do all of these stories mean? What importance do they have to the story of us together, here and now, that is slowly being written?

Answers to questions like these help us build our personal mythology, the hidden structure that supports our storytelling. Psychoanalyst June Singer says, "Personal myths are not what you think they are. They are not false beliefs. They are not the stories you tell yourself to explain your circumstances and behavior. Your personal mythology is, rather, the vibrant infrastructure that informs your life, whether or not you are aware of it. Consciously and unconsciously, you live by your mythology."[1]

Your personal mythology — that infrastructure that informs your life — doesn't exist in a vacuum; it's surrounded by the overarching stories of our culture. Those larger cultural stories are rooted in areas of activity in society that are interconnected but distinct, areas represented by political, religious, economic, aesthetic, intellectual and relational pursuits. We take these cultural stories so for granted that we're hardly conscious of them. We simply accept them as reality — the way it is and the way it always has been. The stories stay unarticulated for the most part, something we generally subscribe to but probably couldn't explain, and something to not bother thinking too much about in a world where there is plenty to hold our attention.

When one of these cultural stories becomes dominant, a master story emerges. That master story begins to change the other cultural stories, and as that larger context begins to shift, your personal mythology — that vibrant infrastructure that informs your life — shifts along with it. A new governing pattern evolves. A monoculture begins to form.

So how do we learn to see that monoculture? How do we learn to see something as pervasive, invisible, and life-forming as air? We can see what effect the monoculture has when we look at what we tell each other about how we and the world ought to be. What is life about? What stories are we told and what stories do we live by?

In these early decades of the twenty-first century, the master story is economic; economic beliefs, values and assumptions are shaping how we think, feel, and act. The beliefs, values and assumptions that make up the economic story aren't inherently right or wrong; they're just a single perspective on the nature of reality. In a monoculture though, that single perspective becomes so engrained as the only reasonable reality that we begin to forget our other stories, and fail to see the monoculture in its totality, never mind question it. We accept it as true simply because we've heard its story so often and live immersed in it day after day. The extent to which we accept that monoculture unquestioningly and live by its tenets is the extent to which our lives are unconsciously being shaped by it.

The first assumption most people make when they learn the monoculture is economic is that the master story is all about money — how to get it, make more of it, spend it, grow it, or keep it, whether that looks like consumerism, commercialism, or materialism. But that's only true of the economic monoculture at a surface level. Though the monoculture naturally embodies issues surrounding money, the economic story represents a much more nuanced and insidious tapestry of beliefs and assumptions that fall into three categories: who you are as a human being, what the world is like, and how you and that world interact.

In the economic story, human nature takes on a particular quality. The story has much to say about what you're like as a human being — what motivates you, what your goals are, and how you think. It then tries to understand and predict your behavior based on that version of your intrinsic nature.

To begin with, in the economic story, you are an individual. John Donne may have said, "No man is an island," but in the economic story you fundamentally exist apart from others. Though you belong to at least one group in practice, since you were born into a family, the economic story doesn't think of you as a group member with group obligations and responsibilities. Instead, it thinks of you as an individual, as someone who is independent of others. As you'll see in the following chapters, that ends up having certain ramifications.

The economic story also says that as a human being, you're rational. In economic thought, being rational doesn't mean that you're sensible or that you're a clear thinker. Being rational means that when you're faced with a decision, you move through a three-stage process to decide what to do. Assuming you know what your goals are, you first lay out all the ways you could reach each goal and identify the costs and benefits of each possibility. Next, you analyze which option is most efficient — the one that most directly lets you get the most of what you want while costing you the least of your resources. Finally, you choose that most efficient option, because in the economic story, your best choice is always the most efficient choice. That means your best choice is never going to be the scenic route or an option that's more extravagant than it needs to be.[2]

In the economic story, you're someone who is self-interested, in the most positive sense possible. Being self-interested is not the same as being selfish. Selfishness involves focusing on yourself to the exclusion of, or at the expense of others. Self-interest, on the other hand, is about doing what you want and working to improve your condition or your situation. The economic story says that as someone who is self-interested, every time you make a decision, you constantly calculate what is and is not to your best advantage in a particular situation.[3]

Being cast as someone who is rational and self-interested might sound relatively harmless, but that way of thinking has implications because it's based on the assumptions that you know what condition you're in, you know what your options are, and you know what you want, but those assumptions don't necessarily hold. For one, it's easy to go wrong in identifying all of your available choices. The economist Tibor Scitovsky compared being able to analyze your options in a given situation to being handed a long menu in a Chinese restaurant. Given all those dishes to choose from, the economic story says you know what pleases you most and so you're going to order what you really want; from the outside looking in, we then assume that your behavior is an expression of your preferences. But Scitovsky says most of us don't understand ninety percent of what's on that menu and so we end up ordering the same thing we always do, or order something new and maybe don't prefer it at all.[4] It's also easy to miss taking important information into account when you're making a decision, and we're not necessarily all that rational to begin with — so much so that some economists now argue that we act irrationally and make wrong decisions systematically.[5] Even so, the economic story says that as a human being, you're rational and self-interested.

The story says that you act as you do because you're trying to get what you want, and the rest of us can tell what you want by watching how you act. If you buy a blue shirt, we assume you must have wanted a blue shirt. If you buy ice cream, we assume you wanted ice cream. *What you want* doesn't really matter in the economic story; the story doesn't have anything to say about the *content* of your preferences. If you want to lose weight by starving yourself or by eating broccoli and walking more, that's up to you. You are the sole and final authority on your preferences, and your behavior is an expression of those preferences.[6] Though what you want and prefer can be shaped by advertising, tradition, a changing context, or your own experience, the economic story maintains that you know yourself, you know what you prefer, and you know whether or not you were satisfied with what you chose the last time.[7] That may not always be true, but that's how the story goes.

In the economic story, you're to think and act like an entrepreneur. Jean-Baptiste Say, a French economist credited with coming up with the term *entrepreneur,* said entrepreneurs are people who shift resources from one place to another to create higher productivity and greater yield. If you're an entrepreneur or are acting entrepreneurially, you are increasing productivity and profits and adding value wherever you go.[8]

You're also someone who can never get enough. Your wants are unlimited, and you're motivated to try to satisfy those unlimited wants even though you'll never be able to. Because you can't get enough of what you really want, you're driven by only one thing: the desire for satisfaction.[9] (Psychologists tend to believe that your motivations are a lot more complicated and subtle than that, but that's another story.) Since everyone has unlimited wants just like you, there isn't enough of anything to go around. Resources, in other words, are scarce.

And that leads us to what the world is like.

In the economic story, the world is made of markets.[10] Those markets are full of people like you and me who are buying and selling goods and services. Sometimes you're a buyer and sometimes you're a seller. What happens in the market depends on whether you're buying or selling.

If you're a seller in the world of markets, the economic story says you're a small enterprise trying to make a profit. You might be a merchant at a local farmers market. Along with all the other merchants, you sell your wares: fresh vegetables and flowers, sausages and cookies, canned goods, or handmade crafts. If there's a run on what you sell, you can raise your asking price. If no one's buying, you'll have to lower it. The price, in other words, is set by the forces of supply and demand — not you. As the story goes, as a seller you're not powerful enough to influence prices.

The same story holds true for wages: the price for your work is also set by the forces of supply and demand. If you don't think you get paid enough, your boss isn't to blame — it's the market that's at fault. Your boss doesn't set your wages — the market does. If help is hard to find, you'll be paid more. If everyone's looking for a job, you'll be paid less. That's because all things being equal, your boss is also considered to be rational. That means your boss will also make the most efficient choice and hire someone appropriate who costs the least of his or her limited resources.

If you end up suffering in the world of markets because prices are too high for you to buy, or too low for you to make a living off of what you sell, there's nobody to blame but the market, which after all, isn't trying to punish you personally.[11] That's just the way things are. So even though giant retailers and multinational energy companies and global technology firms are all big enough and powerful enough to influence prices and wages, the economic story says otherwise.

If you're a buyer in the world of markets, whether you know it or not, you help to keep the market in check. As you browse tables as a buyer at the farmers market, merchants are busy competing with each other for your business. Because you are rational as a buyer, all things being equal, you will buy the most efficient alternative — what meets your needs and uses the least of your resources to do it. The more efficient the seller can be in supplying that product to you, the lower the price can be, which makes you more likely to buy. The economic story says the market is regulated by that kind of competition for buyers and so doesn't need to be regulated further by anything external to it, like the government.

Just as buyers and sellers are efficient in the economic story, so too is the world of markets. When buyers are efficient, buying what meets their needs for as little as possible, and sellers are efficient, making the best product they can for as little as possible, buyers will demand more and sellers will supply more. When there's a balance between supply and demand, the market operates at peak efficiency. Sellers won't produce too much of what they sell, and buyers won't pay for what they don't need, so there ends up being a natural match between what sellers offer and what buyers want. That kind of efficiency, the story says, keeps everyone from wasting resources, which as you'll remember, are scarce because everyone has unlimited wants and there isn't enough of anything to go around. Peak efficiency in the world of markets is reached when both markets and the competition that happens in them are as widespread as possible throughout the world, which is an argument for free trade.

The economic story says there are no limits to how big the world of markets can be, or to how much it can grow. In practice, we keep some things outside of markets, like sex, reproductive services, human organs, political office, prizes and honors, love and friendship, drugs, and homicide. Keeping those areas of life separate from markets means it is mostly illegal to buy and sell sex, children, kidneys, senate seats, Nobel prizes, cocaine, or hits on someone you'd like to see dead — even if there are people who are willing to buy and sell those things.[12] Still, the economic story says the market should operate without limits, which leads us to how you and the world of markets interact.

According to the economic story, you're free to enter and exit the world of markets as you please. As a buyer, you're free to choose whether to buy something or not. If you want something and can afford to pay for it, it's yours. If nothing pleases you, you can "vote with your dollar" and buy nothing. In practice, if you're less mobile than others in the world of markets somehow, maybe because you're a child or a senior, or are poor, or have learning disabilities or mental health issues, you don't have the same access to the market as others do who are more independent. Instead, you'll likely find it hard to identify your choices and make the best choice, which you need to be able to do for the market to operate efficiently, or you may not have enough money to enter the market to begin with. Sometimes your "best choice" isn't much of a choice at all; if your two options are to starve or to buy bread at extortion rates from the only seller in town, your "freedom" to enter or exit the market doesn't amount to much.

The economic story recognizes that "freedom of choice" limitation and says that the more choice you have as a buyer in the market, the better off you are. The story says you're most free when you have as much choice as possible in as many areas of life as possible.[13] Choice means that competition exists, and in the economic story, competition is good. Without competition, prices won't operate the way they're supposed to and the world of markets stagnates. That's why price-fixing is illegal and monopolies aren't that desirable, at least from a buyer's perspective.

Competition is also important on a personal level in the economic story. As a rational, self-interested individual, you interact with the world of markets by competing with everyone else. You compete against other workers for jobs. You compete against other buyers for what sellers are selling. You compete against other sellers for buyers. No matter what role you play in the world of markets, you are competing for a piece of a pie that just isn't big enough to go around. Because resources are scarce, you have to make choices about what you want and then compete with everyone else for what little there is. You can tell how you're doing in the competition by comparing yourself with others. Who's behind you? Who's ahead? The further out in front you are, the better.

Your relationships with others in the world of markets are therefore primarily competitive ones, but they're also typically impersonal and transactional — a relationship between buyer and seller. You don't have to be friends with people or know them at all to do business with them. In a given transaction between two rational, self-interested human beings, you are not obligated to the other person past the transaction at hand.

According to the economic story, your personal experience in the world of markets will be affected by the quality of information you have about what's being offered in the market. The better your information is, the better off you are. With perfect information, you'll be able to make the best decision — the most efficient one — and buy what meets your needs for the lowest available price, because you're rational. No one, of course, ever has perfect information. What you have instead are information asymmetries: potential employees often know more about their real skills than an interviewer does, real estate agents often know more about a property than a house buyer does, and doctors often know more about a medical problem than a sick person does. Information asymmetries make it hard to figure out what your best choice really is; the more information you have, the story says, the better choice you'll be able to make.

In the economic story, life gets better when the economy grows. The economy is deemed to be growing and life is deemed to be improving when the value of a country's economic output — its Gross Domestic Product (GDP) — is rising. When GDP is rising, the story says, your standard of living is going up, your country's income per person is going up, and your children will end up having more opportunities than you had. Health care gets funded. Education gets funded. The arts get funded. Social programs get funded. In short, economic growth enables social growth.

Many observers have pointed out that economic growth doesn't quite tell the whole story; whether growth is good or not depends on exactly what's growing. If crime is on the rise in your neighborhood, and you buy a gun and hire a bodyguard because you no longer feel safe walking down the street, the spike in gun sales and bodyguard services increases the GDP and grows the economy — so though your standard of living may officially be going up, your quality of life is not. But in the economic story, a growing economy is seen as an unequivocally good thing.

To summarize then, in the economic story, you're a rational, self-interested, entrepreneurial individual who is trying to satisfy unlimited wants, whatever they may be. The world is a world of markets populated with buyers and sellers. Prices are set by the forces of supply and demand, so power is in the market, not in people, and cannot be personally directed. In the world of markets, sellers strive for profits and buyers buy what costs them the least of their resources. The world is regulated by competition for buyers and is efficient, so scarce resources aren't wasted. Peak efficiency is reached when markets and competition are as widespread as possible, and market size and market growth know no limits. When you interact with that world of markets, you are free to come and go as you please. The more choice you have, the better; choice stimulates competition, and without competition, markets won't work. The more information you have, the better decisions you'll make. You compete with everyone and everyone competes with you. Relationships are impersonal, anonymous and transactional, and economic growth enables social growth.

Now that we know how the economic story positions who we are as human beings, what the world is like, and how we and the world interact, we're ready to look at how that story plays out in daily life, creating a monoculture that ultimately constrains us.

You're about to discover how different elements of the economic story are being adopted, or have already been adopted, in interdependent but distinct parts of life that were once governed by a much wider range of ideas. In the next six chapters, you'll start to see the economic story in action. You'll see how the story's assumptions are changing how you think and act in terms of your work, your relationships with people and the natural world, your community, your physical and spiritual health, your education, and your creativity.

You'll start to see how one story is changing everything.

3

YOUR WORK

It is not correct to say that we managed to maintain employment during the depression because we grew. We grew because we had committed ourselves to the maintenance of employment. This forced us to find new users and new uses for our existing products...I sometimes wonder whether we wouldn't be well advised to commit ourselves to increasing employment constantly.

—IBM EXECUTIVE, 1954

If the world operates as one big market, every employee will compete with every person anywhere in the world who is capable of doing the same job. There are a lot of them and many of them are very hungry.

—ANDREW GROVE, INTEL PRESIDENT AND CEO, 1995

Would I ever leave this company? Look, I'm all about loyalty. In fact, I feel like part of what I'm being paid for here is my loyalty. But if there were somewhere else that valued loyalty more highly, I'm going wherever they value loyalty the most.

—DWIGHT SCHRUTE, *THE OFFICE*, 2005

IF YOU WERE EMPLOYED full-time in the 1950s, you expected to work about 40 hours a week. Your job security stretched out into the future indefinitely. Monday to Friday, you'd show up at your boss' place of business, and do mostly what your boss told you to. You knew what your job entailed because it had specific tasks attached to it. Your work was supervised. You moved from position to position within the company, climbing the promotion ladder. Layoffs, when they happened, were based on seniority: last in, first out. Shareholders, not employees, were the ones who took the risk for how business decisions turned out. Your pay and your performance weren't really tied together. If you and your coworkers were paid for high performance at all, it wasn't used to differentiate among you much.[1] And, most working people were just like you. Though only about 20 percent of the population worked for wages and salaries in 1820, and 50 percent did by 1900, by 2000, well over 90 percent worked for organizations, and half of those worked for big companies.[2]

Back in the 1950s, the relationship between employees and their companies involved commitment and reciprocity; workers were committed to the job in return for wages and promotions, and the company was committed to its workers in return for their hard work and loyalty. Firms invested in training employees and developing their skills, and promoted people from within the firm. That long-term employment relationship, with its stability, regular promotions, and raises, let employees plan on owning a home and sending their children to college or university. In exchange, workers were loyal and didn't move around much, staying with the same company in the same city for years, maybe even decades.[3] If people occasionally had to work long hours, the impact was relatively easy to absorb; whatever didn't get done at home was usually taken care of by women who weren't out in the workforce — mothers, grandmothers, wives, sisters, or daughters.

Then the story changed.

The economic story tells us corporations compete in a global market as part of the global economy. Because investors are always on the lookout for where to invest their capital next and keep moving their funds in and out of countries, organizations are under pressure to compete efficiently and stay attractive to those investors.[4] One way a company can compete efficiently is to have a more flexible workforce — to be less tied to its employees. Since labor costs represent a major expense to most companies, hiring employees when there's work and laying them off when the work slows down can help firms stay competitive. That means the employment relationship that once stretched out into the future isn't on the table anymore. Jobs now depend on the changing needs of the company. If the company has work, so will you. If not, you probably won't either.

As a result, corporations and employees are no longer that committed to each other. Companies have gradually started limiting job security and now invest less in training employees than they used to while still expecting workers to show dedication to their jobs. Employees, on the other hand, are becoming more mobile; if a competing company approached them, they'd think seriously about switching firms. Employees now also worry about taking care of their own training and skill development to make sure they stay attractive to potential employers. Many workers expect to go back to school to get that training, which costs them time and money. Still, without training, they're at risk of falling behind because they won't have the credentials others do in a competitive job market.

Those workers who do end up laid off when the work slows down might be able to get hired back as consultants or contractors. According to the economic story, being part of that kind of flexible workforce is a great opportunity for workers: being a free agent means you'll finally be able to end the absurd, dysfunctional long-term relationship between you and your company. You'll be more secure; having multiple clients is safer than working for just one boss. You'll make more money. Your work will be more invigorating, more rewarding, more fun. You'll finally surface your submerged identity, figure out who you are and what you really want to do with your life. You'll find yourself, finally believe in yourself, become authentic and whole.[5]

You also won't be alone; contingent work is still on the rise in North America, Europe and Asia. But we now know that free agents often end up making *less* money than they did in their full-time jobs and have fewer benefits like health insurance and a pension.[6] Some free agents try to make up lost wages by taking a second job, then end up spending less time with family and friends; researchers studying the effects of contingent work said they saw "real signs of social *disintegration*, a weakening of the social fabric of these individuals' lives."[7]

Job security and long-term employment aside, the economic story is also changing how companies talk about their relationship to the rest of society in terms of corporate social responsibility. Businesses exist to make money, to be sure — that's their traditional purpose, compared to organizations like churches and hospitals.[8] But corporate social responsibility is also gaining attention, along with related ideas like sustainable development and social audits. Corporations have started talking about *stakeholders* — people affected by the company's decisions who can't just be ignored when the company is trying to decide what course of action to pursue. Ethicist Richard De George wrote: "The present mandate [between business and society] is different from the simplistic mandate given to business in an earlier time…What is clear in the new mandate is that business must now consider the worker, consumer, and the general public as well as the shareholder — and the views and demands of all four — in making decisions. The good of all must be considered."[9] *Stakeholders* want results too, just like shareholders, but those results aren't automatically measured in dollars and cents. Profits, while necessary, now aren't sufficient.

That changing social mandate and emphasis on stakeholders means companies and their employees are supposed to move from focusing on the financial bottom line to focusing on a triple bottom line of economic, social, and environmental responsibility. Both economic and non-economic factors are supposed to be taken into account in corporate decision-making.

But in the economic story, the non-economic factors companies are supposed to take into account are reframed in terms of the bottom line again; companies can *do well by doing good.*[10] According to that philosophy, companies that "do good" by acting ethically also end up "doing well" financially. In other words, ethics pays.[11] As one public relations expert put it, "There is strong evidence that companies that institutionalize values and codes of conduct be they related to the environment, working conditions, privacy — are rewarded with higher stock valuations, better earnings, and a more highly motivated and satisfied workforce — evidence that doing good is not just good for business, it's good for the soul. There is even a growing belief that social responsibility is so important to corporate reputation that it should be valued and recognized as a real corporate asset as with any important item on an asset balance sheet."[12]

The economic story also says that corporate citizenship needs to be justified in economic terms. A healthy psychological workplace is worth developing — not because we value mental health at work, but because it improves organizational performance.[13] Work/family balance programs are worth setting up — not because we believe in helping employees manage work/family conflict, but because the programs increase employee commitment to the organization.[14] Worker wellness programs are worthwhile — not because we value health in and of itself, but because healthy workers are productive workers, and the company's Medicare costs have to be reduced.[15]

Even the concept of sustainable development has been reframed. In the economic story, sustainable development no longer refers to corporate activity that's sustainable in terms of the environment, but to activity that's sustainable in terms of the corporation. Sustainable development is about doing what's required to sustain corporate growth and profits. The economic story, in other words, reroutes that triple bottom line back to the economic bottom line.

So what happens when ethics doesn't pay? What happens when acting ethically *costs* us? Whistleblowers are typically fired for reporting corporate wrongdoing. They rarely get their jobs back and often never work in the field again. "An average fate," says scholar C. Fred Alford, "is for a nuclear engineer to end up selling computers at Radio Shack."[16]

Still, the economic story insists that you can have your cake and eat it too, that the trade-off between ethics and profits is just an illusion. As a Royal Dutch Shell sustainability report states, "We hope, through this report and by our future actions, to show that the basic interests of business and society are entirely compatible — that there does not have to be a choice between profits and principles."[17] No one has to make a decision between going one way or another when all roads lead to Rome.

For many, though, that conflict between profits and principles still exists. Management professor Peter Pruzan facilitated a workshop for the executives of a company known for hierarchical control and an emphasis on shareholders, not stakeholders. Pruzan gave these executives, flown in from eight Western countries, a list of 'values' like success, love, professional competency, honesty, trust, wealth, creativity and power and asked them to reflect on which ones were most important in their personal lives. They were to discuss their selections in small groups and then list the group's top five personal values. Later that day, the executives were asked to reflect on the *company's* most important values — not the ones officially promoted, but the implicit ones underlying decisions about hiring and firing employees, entering and leaving markets, advertising, lobbying, or negotiating with unions.

When the groups compared their lists of personal and corporate values, everyone realized that within each group, the two sets of values were completely different. The executives' personal values tended to include terms like 'good health,' 'honesty,' 'beauty,' 'love,' and 'peace of mind,' and the organizational values included words like 'success,' 'power,' 'competitiveness,' 'efficiency,' and 'productivity.'

Pruzan noted that after that consulting experience, he began to picture the "strongly shareholder-oriented manager" as someone who puts aside his or her personal values at work for the sake of managing, shaping, and organizing, then collects those personal values again at the end of the day and goes home to enjoy beauty, love, friendship, and peace. The gap between a leader's personal values and the values he or she promotes at work is so extreme, Pruzan said, that leaders have unconsciously developed a modern form of schizophrenia, threatening the health of both the leader and the organization.[18]

Employees and executives alike might wish the gap between their personal values and the values of their company were more aligned, but who can be sure value alignment is going to be different anywhere else? Employees learn to keep their heads down and lower their expectations about job security. They start keeping an eye on the door. They think seriously about developing portable skills that can walk out that door with them in case the company sheds them to become more competitive and efficient.

Employees also find themselves working more hours than they once did. In the economic story, it's cheaper for a company to have a worker put in longer hours and do more with less than it is to hire more people; every new hire represents an additional overhead expense. Seventy-seven percent of American workers now work more than 40 hours a week, and less than half of them are "very satisfied" with working conditions in their main paid job. Compared to the countries of the European Union, North Americans report the highest incidence of working at a high speed "all the time," contributing to stress and burnout.[19] The Japanese have a word for "sudden death from overwork": *karoshi*.[20] In China, the word for "overwork death" is *guolaosi*; 600,000 people are estimated to die of it every year.[21]

In America, working long hours used to be the fate of the lowest-paid workers. But by 2002, according to the National Bureau of Economic Research, the highest-paid workers were twice as likely to work long hours as their lowest-paid counterparts.[22] Lawyers are a prime example. When the billable hour was first introduced in law firms (before that, lawyers billed by the task, not the hour), lawyers were expected to bill between 1,200 and 1,500 hours a year. Today they're expected to bill 1,800 to 2,000 hours a year; almost half of practicing lawyers in the United States bill at least 1,900 hours annually. Too, every billable hour involves administrative hours that can't be billed out, so 2,000 billable hours actually translates into 10-11 hour days, 6 days a week, 50 weeks a year.[23]

In addition to having long workdays, lawyers also have four times the depression rate of the general public and twice the substance abuse rate. Two-thirds to three-quarters report high stress, and a third say work stress is hurting their physical and emotional health.[24] But for better or for worse, being willing to work long hours is often about survival in the firm. As the American Bar Association's introductory book *Making Partner* explains to young associates, "If a firm expects a minimum of 1,850 hours, and two associates do equally good work, the associate who bills 2,000 hours will be more valuable to the firm than the associate who bills 1,850 hours. By doing more to help the firm's bottom line, the associate who works harder is demonstrating that he or she is thinking like an owner."[25]

Lawyers aren't the only highly-paid workers facing overwhelming hours. In an interview, Robert Devlin, former president, chairman and CEO of insurance giant American General Corporation, said: "I'm often working eighteen-hour days. I rarely get more than four or five hours a night of sleep. And the way I view it, and I tell the guys, my senior staff, you know, these are seven-day-a-week, twenty-four-hours-a-day jobs. I mean, now, obviously we have our time off and I encourage people to take it. But the fact of the matter is that if a situation pops up and we have to burn up a Saturday or a Sunday and go into, you know, the wee hours of the morning we do so — I mean, I've been in sessions — particularly when you get into mergers and acquisitions where we've walked out of a place at four-thirty in the morning. You kind of have to be prepared to do whatever it takes. If not, you should find something else to do with your time."[26]

Still, working all the time makes it hard for people to keep up with things like childcare, eldercare, house maintenance, cooking, and relationships with friends, family, and significant others. When employees put family ahead of work, they hear about it at work, and when they put work ahead of family, they hear about it at home. Some people are no longer sure they even have time to start a family or add to it.

The economic story, though, says that time crunch, along with your non-work obligations, are your problem as an individual — not your company's problem, or society's problem. It's something you need to solve yourself, however you can. That's so even though, researchers say, the majority of families today are dual-career households and jobs are still being designed as though employees have uninterrupted decades to devote to a career and someone at home full time to look after the domestic side of life.[27]

Chances are, you don't have that kind of time or that kind of life, but it doesn't seem to matter.

That's how the story goes.

4

YOUR RELATIONSHIPS WITH OTHERS AND THE NATURAL WORLD

In our extremely individualistic society we have come to see isolation and loneliness as akin to 'the human condition,' instead of as by-products of a certain kind of social arrangement.

—ROBERT SOLOMON

The leaves at the top, because they are water-stressed, are not doing as much photosynthesis per unit mass…In essence, the plant is investing a certain amount into those tissues but they're not providing as much return on that investment.

—PHYSIOLOGICAL ECOLOGIST, BBC NEWS

WHETHER YOU FEEL CONNECTED to the world or adrift in it, you can't help but be tangled up with other people and the environment. You're born into a family and maybe have one of your own — a significant other, children, parents, brothers and sisters, grandparents, aunts and uncles, cousins, nieces and nephews — people you're connected to whether you like it or not. Your friends, as they say, are the family you choose for yourself. You've got neighbors too, whether you wave at them or pretend you don't see them, people who live around you, or who you run into regularly at the post office, the grocery store, the gym, online. Then there are your colleagues, the people you work with directly and the people you know indirectly through work. You're somehow tied to strangers too by virtue of your shared humanity, those unknown people on the bus or on the other side of the world. Past all of those relationships, you're then related to your physical environment, to wind and water, sun and rain, in urban or rural settings, because wherever you are, you exist in physical space, shaping it and being shaped by it.

Let's start with family. Your kin relationships were once the glue that held society together. Friendships were considered luxuries, but kin relationships were about survival in an uncertain world. Kin were the people who were obligated to help you and who you were obligated to help when catastrophe struck. Being a member of a family meant you had lifetime membership among that group of people, and legal and cultural rights and responsibilities that came with that membership.[1] You were expected to be loyal to your family and they were expected to be loyal to you. Cooperation and trust among family members mattered. In the family, you were judged based on what you needed as a family member and in terms of your intrinsic value — your right to sit at the family table simply because you were a member of the family. You belonged.[2]

Though families and markets have been intertwined throughout history (unless families managed to be completely self-sufficient, which was rare), both were considered separate spheres of activity — so much so that in the 1950s, from a business perspective, family relationships were considered a hindrance to a market mentality and to corporate development.[3] In the Western world, markets were based for the most part on the traditional breadwinner model of the family: a man was paid for working outside the home and a woman wasn't paid for working inside the home. At one time, most families were breadwinner families; in 1900, 94 percent of married American women stayed out of the paid workforce.[4]

In the larger community, your relationships with people were based on values like respect, love, and a willingness to put others first — all of which kept your more self-oriented tendencies in check. Yes, you developed economic relationships through buying and selling with others, but those economic relationships were tempered by the fact that everyone involved in the transaction was considered part of civil society, and civil society was characterized by a basic level of trust and solidarity. Your community, as a group, helped people in need because those struggling were deemed to have inherent dignity and self-worth no matter what their economic situation was like. The goal of the community was to help the destitute become healthy and self-sufficient and to build and strengthen our relationships with each other so we could all function successfully in society together.[5] That's what gave families and communities a higher moral stature than markets.[6]

Nature enjoyed a high moral stature too. Some people valued their relationship with the physical world in terms of their own humanity, believing nature was worth caring for because it contributes to human health, is aesthetically beautiful, or plays a role in shaping their identity, since where people come from can shape who they are. Others valued nature for its own sake, believing they should care for it because other sentient species had a right to live too, or because they respected all life whether it was sentient or not, or for God's sake, because nature represented God's order, God's creation.[7]

Then the story changed.

The economic story says that among your own kind, competition matters more than cooperation, and that you're motivated to look after your own interests, constantly calculating what's in it for you, just like everyone else. Being a member of a group no longer means that you are part of something bigger than yourself. You participate in different groups not for the sake of the group, but to further your own interests. In turn, the group you're part of objectively judges you based on your performance and your worth to them, not on your needs or your intrinsic value as a human being.

Now you're only as good as your last contribution to the team. Your performance or lack of it is what makes you relevant or irrelevant to others. Sociologist Zygmunt Bauman described the phenomenon in terms of reality television: "More than anything else, the...most popular [reality] television shows are public rehearsals of the *disposability* of humans. They carry an indulgence and a warning rolled into one story. No one is indispensable, no one has the right to his or her share in the fruits of the joint effort just because she or he has added at some point to their growth, let alone because of being, simply, a member of the team. Life is a hard game for hard people. Each game starts from scratch, past merits do not count, you are worth only as much as the results of your most recent duel. Each player at the moment is for herself or himself, and to progress, not to mention to reach the top, one must first cooperate in excluding the many who block the way, only to outwit in the end those with whom one cooperated."[8]

Remember, the economic story says you live in a world of markets. As a buyer or seller in those markets, your worth among others is based on your potential or actual ability to contribute to the economy by spending or making money. For the world of markets to operate effectively, you also have to be able to make choices, process information on which to base those choices, and be able to make a new choice if you want to; those hindered by something like a learning disability are therefore "deemed to be of only marginal economic value."[9] The more you drive the economy by making money or spending it, the more desirable you are to others. Your relational ties are primarily economic ties, and so your relationships are transactional. You learn to shun long-term commitments, no longer obligated to anyone past the transaction at hand.

By 2000, 61 percent of married American women worked outside the home for pay, turning the breadwinner model of the family on its head and making dual-earner couples the rule, not the exception.[10] Today, whether you're single or part of a couple, chances are there is no one at home to look after your domestic life, which means you're almost certainly struggling to keep up with everything that's involved in keeping a career and a home going as you work longer and longer hours.

In the meantime, markets keep developing for what used to happen at home for free. You realize you can hire people to cook your meals, care for your children, look after your aging relatives, clean your house, do your tax return, walk the dog, mow the lawn, and prune the shrubs. Outsourcing domestic life helps you cope with the time pressures you're under. Researcher Arlie Russell Hochschild says, "As time becomes something to 'save' at home as much as or even more than at work, domestic life becomes quite literally a second shift; a cult of efficiency, once centered in the workplace, is allowed to set up shop and make itself comfortable at home. Efficiency has become both a means to an end — more home time — and a way of life, an end in itself."[11]

As work and home demand more and more of your time and energy, you may find your significant relationships becoming secondary. It's not that you want to drift away from your spouse, family and close friends, but without spending time and energy on those relationships, they're in danger of fading.[12] In the economic story, rewards in society are based on your performance in your paid job, after all — not on what's going on in the rest of your life.

Even family obligations can weigh on you. Among all of the reasons people give for having fewer children, including religion, ideology, and lifestyle preference, one of them continues to be "time famine."[13] Many think twice about having children or having more of them. Researcher Sylvia Ann Hewlett notes that the typical childless executive woman at midlife has been subject to a "creeping nonchoice" despite the fact that almost 90 percent of high-achieving women want a family. Hewlett explains, "Think of what a 55-hour week means in terms of work-life balance. If you assume an hour lunch and a 45-minute round-trip commute (the national average), the workday stretches to almost 13 hours. Even without 'extras' (out of town trips, client dinners, work functions), this kind of schedule makes it extremely difficult for any professional to maintain a relationship."[14]

In the economic story, children in particular come to represent a real economic risk and cost. Choosing to have a family begins to look like choosing economic vulnerability.[15] "It's not just that people sacrifice their live relationships, and the care of their children, to pursue their careers," says philosopher Charles Taylor. "Something like this has perhaps always existed. The point is that today many people feel *called* to do this, feel they ought to do this, feel their lives would be somehow wasted or unfulfilled if they didn't do it."[16]

"In a word," says economist Stephen Marglin, "markets are the cutting edge of the loss of human connection."[17] Most economists, he adds, see that loss of human connection as a virtue; markets are more efficient than communities, which valued friendliness, community spirit, and a willingness to work on behalf of the community without expecting to be paid. As markets develop for what used to happen in families for free, the caring that happened at home is slowly transferred to larger, more impersonal institutions. The cost of care goes up, not least because it had nowhere to go but up since women working at home weren't being paid for what they did. That rising cost of care is good news if you're someone who wasn't being paid for the care you were giving, but not so good if you're someone who needs care and who can't afford to pay for it. But even if you can afford to pay for it, money doesn't guarantee that the care you get is going to be high quality.[18]

The economic story says that getting involved in your community is a constraint and an obligation. Your parents or grandparents might have stayed in one neighborhood — even one house — for thirty, forty, or fifty years, and known everyone within shouting distance. Psychologist Mary Pipher wrote: "There is pleasure in just acknowledging each other, in nodding on the street and chatting in the cafés and grocery stores. To move away from a true home is to move away from life. I don't think we begin to acknowledge and understand how much we have lost."[19]

But in the economic story, staying put is not ideal. Being mobile is preferred because mobility enables economic development. The more mobile you are, the story says, the more access you'll have to jobs, education, services, and social activities.[20] Even marriage doesn't have to keep you in the same city as your spouse anymore. Couples in commuter marriages live apart during the week to pursue their individual careers in different cities and maintain their relationship over the phone or through weekend flights "home." You need to stay loose, be ready to pick up and go, though that makes it harder for you to put down roots and develop close, long-term relationships.[21]

Those close, long-term relationships, though, aren't what they once were either. In the economic story, friends, neighbors, people in your community, and even strangers, whether in person or online, are all potential members of the audience you're building for whatever it is you do as you strive to develop your personal brand. As business author Tom Peters put it, "When you're promoting brand You, everything you do — and everything you choose not to do — communicates the value and character of the brand. Everything from the way you handle phone conversations to the email messages you send to the way you conduct business in a meeting is part of the larger message you're sending about your brand."[22]

Your relationships are transactional — a means to an end, not an end in themselves. What matters is building a bigger audience. If you can connect with the right people, the people with the biggest audiences themselves, you never know what someone might be able to do for you or how you might be able to monetize those connections in the future. German sociologist Ferdinand Tönnies called that type of association *Gesellschaft*, a connection created to promote the interests of its members, where people who are essentially separate come together for a period of togetherness because it is to their benefit to do so. Tönnies then contrasted that association with *Gemeinschaft*, on the other hand, which occurs when people are essentially united even though they may be occasionally separate, where the ties between them, like family ties, exist whether they are advantageous or not.[23]

In terms of your community, the economic story says that you can care for the needy and create social change by taking an entrepreneurial or business-based approach to social issues. That kind of activity, called social entrepreneurship, is about trying to make markets work for people. Social entrepreneurs add value (social value in this case) by offering new products and services that are supposed to ultimately meet social needs, or by developing social programs that produce some kind of significant social return.[24] Not-for-profit organizations are told to develop revenue streams so they can make money and rely less on donations and public funding, even though critics warn that becoming business-oriented can be dangerous, that operating a not-for-profit organization as a business can undermine the organization's social mission.[25] Even so, a report from the Kellogg Foundation notes that nonprofits "are using entrepreneurial models and language to design their services, organizations, and partnerships...There are hundreds — and perhaps thousands — of examples throughout the United States of organizations that are experimenting with enterprise or market-based approaches for solving problems. Many of these are based within traditional organizations such as Goodwill, Salvation Army, Boy and Girl Scouts, community food banks, etc."[26]

According to the former Chief Marketing Officer and Managing Director Corporate Opportunities of the Boys & Girls Club of America (B&GCA), the organization is practicing social entrepreneurship by developing "mutually beneficial" marketing alliances with corporate partners. The alliances are based on the idea that the B&GCA brand is worth something to a corporation and can help it achieve its goals. B&GCA has developed alliances with Coca-Cola worth $60 million, and alliances with JCPenney ($7 million), Circuit City ($3 million), Crest/P&G ($3.3 million), Compaq ($7.5 million), Microsoft ($100 million), The Sports Authority ($3.3 million), and others.[27]

In the economic story, traditional philanthropy doesn't work, but if you cross charity with the principles behind venture capital, you get something even better — venture philanthropy. Venture philanthropists aren't donors who fund grant proposals — they're investors who invest in business plans. From this point of view, investment is more effective than charity; emerging venture philanthropists "don't want to hear about the have-nots and the negativity associated with this dependency syndrome."[28] Market concepts should be used to design social goods and services. Programs funded shouldn't be evaluated at some future date — their performance should be measured, and they ought to demonstrate innovation, measurable outcomes, and tangible results. Venture philanthropists can calculate their social return on investment by quantifying things like how much income tax revenue is generated by a homeless person who gets a paying job; the higher the return, the better the investment.[29]

The economic story also tells us that venture philanthropists ought to manage the relationship between themselves and the not-for-profit organizations they invest in. They can provide management expertise as well as cash, maybe get a seat on the board, monitor the organization's performance and make it accountable for results, then develop an exit strategy that's based on the organization becoming self-sufficient. Research suggests, though, that the U.S. nonprofit sector's adoption of market values and methods has weakened democracy and citizenship — weakened the ability of those organizations to create and maintain a strong civil society. The market's emphasis on being entrepreneurial and satisfying customers is incompatible with the sector's traditional emphasis on citizenship, collective action for the public interest, and the democratic ideals of fairness and justice.[30] Nevertheless, venture philanthropists are to throw their support behind programs that focus first on economic and educational improvement, believing that spiritual and social wealth will follow.[31]

One form of shared wealth that is critically important in the economic story is the environment. The story tells us that we ought to value the natural world because the environment is literally worth money. Biodiversity is natural capital — a storehouse of economic resources that exists for our benefit, something we can literally put a price tag on. Mother Earth is a service provider who provides life-fulfilling and life-sustaining ecosystem services. Those ecosystems, including the species of which the ecosystems are made, are delivered to all of us free of charge.[32] Ecosystems like the polar regions matter because they give us commercially valuable fish, provide food, shelter, clothing and tools from the caribou, give us fuels from wood, sod and peat, and turn on the "global air-conditioning." The oceans and seas matter because they represent a renewable energy potential and a desalinated water supply, regulate the climate, provide protein for one billion people, give us sea sponges from which we make fibre-optic technology, and facilitate the shipping and transport means for 90 percent of our international trade in goods.[33]

Because nature's ecosystems provide us with so many goods and services for free, in the economic story, the loss of those systems represents an enormous financial liability. The best way then, to demonstrate just how much these ecosystems are worth is to price them out so we can see how much it costs us when nature is destroyed. In Germany, a meeting of the G8+5 Environment Ministers in 2007 led to a global study on the economics of the loss of biodiversity and ecosystem degradation. The study highlighted countries saving or making money from conservation efforts. In Venezuela, "investment in the national protected area system is preventing sedimentation that otherwise could reduce farm earnings by around U.S.$3.5 million a year. Planting and protecting nearly 12,000 hectares of mangroves in Vietnam costs just over $1 million but saved annual expenditures on dyke maintenance of well over $7 million…Investment in the protection of Guatemala's Maya Biosphere Reserve is generating an annual income of close to $50 million a year, created 7,000 jobs, and boosted local family incomes."[34] The Natural Capital Project — a collaboration of The Nature Conservancy, the World Wildlife Fund, and Stanford University's Woods Institute for the Environment — is looking "for practical ways to quantify the seemingly unquantifiable: What is the dollar value of a wetland? Can you put a price tag on a rainforest and the many services it provides humanity?"[35] One of the project's internationally renowned scientists says, "Our goal is…to show how one can actually get a really high return on investing in living natural capital through conservation."[36]

In other words, the economic story tells us we ought to save nature because it *pays* to save it. In economic terms, it's win-win. The story doesn't concern itself with what happens if it *costs* us to save our environment. How will we justify sparing a rainforest or protecting a species from extinction if it's literally worth more to cut the forest down or to let the species die? Still, in the economic story, "If you want to save the Amazon, go to business school and learn how to do a deal."[37]

5

YOUR COMMUNITY

Government is instituted for the common good; for the protection, safety, prosperity, and happiness of the people; and not for profit, honor, or private interest of any one man, family, or class of men.
—JOHN ADAMS, U.S. PRESIDENT, 1776

The biggest challenge is going to be how to best utilize taxpayer dollars to the benefit of industry.
—MIKE SMITH, U.S. DEPARTMENT OF ENERGY, 2002

FOR ALMOST AS LONG as we've been coming together in groups and sorting out how to get along, we've regulated how we live together in community through different levels of government. When the economic story spreads through your community and into your government, it changes how the government understands itself and makes decisions on your behalf, which means it also ends up profoundly changing arm's-length government organizations like prisons and public libraries.

Before the economic story began to spread, we lived together and governed ourselves based on the assumption that the public and private sectors served different purposes. The public sector operated in the public interest, developing and investing in public goods like health, education, and safety for the good of the community. The private sector, at the other end of the spectrum, operated for monetary gain. The two sectors were even governed by different bodies of law: constitutional and administrative law for the public sector, and corporate law for the private sector.

Public servants subscribed to a set of values that came to be known as the public service ethos. According to that ethos, public officials were ideally to be law-abiding citizens of upright and honest character who were accountable to the democratic process, loyal to the common good, and impartial and fair in their treatment of others — no special favors for friends and higher-ups.[1]

Civil servants carried out the work of the government and were answerable to it. The government, being democratic, was in turn answerable to you, the public, so the whole system was ultimately answerable to the people. That public service ethos gave us a vision of political life as a noble calling, a life lived in dedication to the public good and in service to your community and country. Not everybody in public service lived up to that ideal, but the ideal existed, and people aspired to it.

Then the story changed.

In the 1970s and 1980s, researchers began to notice that governments in Australia, Canada, New Zealand, the United Kingdom, and the United States had shifted from using one set of values and practices to another. The basic difference between these two ways .of doing and being government (one called Public Administration and the other called New Public

Management) revolved around whether or not the public and private sectors really were distinct. Public Administration said yes, the sectors were different and ought to be managed differently. New Public Management said no, the sectors weren't distinct, and that the tools and techniques of the private sector could be used to manage the public sector too. In this way, the rise of New Public Management in government represents the spread of the economic story.[2]

The economic story says that the public sector is rife with problems: it's inefficient and ineffective, wastes money by not controlling costs, has low standards of quality, lets its employees have too much influence through trade unions and professional associations, and so makes citizens unhappy. Civil servants and politicians aren't responding to a noble calling of service to community and country — instead, they are rational, self-interested individuals just like the rest of us. Civil servants are entrepreneurial and want to maximize their departmental budgets. Politicians, on the other hand, want to maximize their chances of reelection.[3]

Given all of these problems in the public sector, the economic story says the solution is to run government like a business. Citizens become customers. Governments start to focus on what businesses focus on: improving quality and performance, cutting costs, being productive, providing better customer service, being more responsive to customers, and benchmarking against best practices. Cost control and performance improvement supersede the old philosophy of development and investment for the public good. Competition is introduced into government through outsourcing, deregu-

lation, privatization, and commercialization, in order to make
government effective and responsive and therefore worthy of
your support.[4]

According to the economic story, civil servants who once
provided public services in-house should outsource that work
to the private sector and supervise the delivery of those services instead.[5] But because the private sector is not answerable
to the democratic process, that outsourcing raises concerns
that community, democracy, and the public interest are being
eroded as the public service ethos fades.[6]

As the economic story spreads in government, a language
based on economics develops along with a new way of thinking and reasoning about what goes on in government — a
kind of accounting logic.[7] That accounting logic makes two
assumptions; first, that anything and everything your government does can be assessed in terms of what value is added,
and second, that the value added can be linked to how much
money is spent on the activity in the first place. An accounting logic says that if a program or action is worth more than
it costs, it is a good investment and worth doing. If it is worth
less, it is a bad investment and not worth repeating.

On the surface of things, an accounting logic seems neutral and objective, independent and fair — a way of comparing
numbers to numbers. In reality, it's less than straightforward.
Public goods like health, education, literacy, and security are
notoriously difficult to measure. If your city decides to set
aside green space for a park, what is that park worth, in dollars? And how is that number arrived at exactly?

An accounting logic can also be used to indirectly control what civil servants do. By evaluating their work in terms of value-added, an accounting logic weakens professional independence and skews civil servants' behavior toward what they are being evaluated for. (If your performance review is suddenly based on how many paperclips you can link together, you will probably start linking together paperclips.) But what professionals do — the "outputs" that the accounting logic wants to measure — has never been easy to assess or even to compare from person to person to begin with.[8]

Nevertheless, by 2000, New Public Management was recognized as the main paradigm being used by governments around the world even though no one was sure whether governments were actually becoming more efficient and effective as promised or not.[9] In the economic story though, values like efficiency and effectiveness are equivalent to the common good. The question, "What should we do?" comes to have one answer: "Whatever is efficient."[10] That philosophy changes how governments think and act.

Government is the only body in society that's legally allowed to use force and coercion against you in order to keep the social order. If you break the law, it's the government that can take away your freedom and sometimes even your life as part of its exercise of authority. In America, when you're convicted of a crime, the government takes away your freedom by sending you to prison.

Prisons have existed for thousands of years — once used only sporadically though because of the expense — but gov-

ernments haven't always been involved in punishing crime. In
the Middle Ages in England, crime was thought to concern
only the criminal and the victim, not the criminal and the
rest of society, so government, representing society's interests,
didn't have a role to play. Blood feuds developed as a result, but
even so, the tradition of non-government intervention lasted
until the 1800s.[11]

It wasn't until the Enlightenment that crime became
thought of as something that affected all of society and not
just the victim. Crime became a public issue, an offence
against the state that now had to be handled by the state's
officials.[12] Governments protected the public and the public
interest by sending criminals to prison as retribution (because
they deserved it), deterrence (so they wouldn't do it again),
incapacitation (so they couldn't do it again), or reform and
rehabilitation (changing behavior and attitudes).[13]

All of that government activity cost money, and during
the 1800s, the government started contracting out prisoners
as workers across America, sometimes into appalling conditions; slave labor was disappearing after abolition, and prison
labor was seen as a substitute for it. The practice of contracting
out prisoners as workers was widespread. In 1825, the state of
Kentucky, in financial crisis, leased its prisoners to a business-
man for $1,000 a year for five years. New York's Sing Sing had
its prisoners work in marble quarries. Other prisons had their
occupants make shoes, clothes, carpets, or furniture to help
defray the public cost of crime.[14] Contracting prisoners out
served two purposes: prisons started making the government

money instead of costing it, and work, said the Protestant work ethic, could itself be used to reform a prisoner's character.

Not everyone was happy with the arrangement. Unions and manufacturers complained that prison labor undercut the work of free men and entrepreneurs. Too, prison conditions ended up being so bad and inmate exploitation so widespread that public agencies were eventually forced to assume responsibility for prisons.[15] Leasing convicts out as workers ended in 1923, and contracting prisoners out to private firms had mostly disappeared by 1940. Prison became an expensive proposition for government again.[16]

In the 1970s, those costs worsened; America's prison population doubled. The practice of contracting out prisoners was restarted. Then, in the 1980s and 1990s era of tough sentencing, stringent political attitudes, and the "war on crime", the prison population doubled again. By early 1992, the United States had the highest number of people incarcerated per capita in the world. Federal and state prison operating costs jumped from $3.1 billion in 1980 to over $17 billion in 1994 — an increase of almost 550 percent based on inflation-adjusted dollars.[17]

Both government and the public loathed the financial burden that prisons represented. In the economic story, one solution to skyrocketing costs is to introduce competition and outsource operations, either piecemeal or in their entirety. As costs rose, the prison management services offered by cost-cutting private firms started to look more attractive.

Corporations were already involved in the justice system anyway through drug treatment centers, electronic surveillance, halfway houses, juvenile detention centers, work programs in adult prisons, and food and laundry services. Outsourcing adult prisons in their entirety simply represented the next level of private sector involvement.[18]

Advocates said outsourcing prison management would cut costs by about 20 percent and that corporations couldn't possibly do a worse job of running prisons than the government, what with overcrowding, ballooning expenses and lousy living conditions. Private prisons would be cheaper, more efficient, and more responsive, offering better security, better food, and better medical care.[19] Critics questioned whether corporations should be allowed to be responsible for the lives and freedom of prisoners and to profit from their suffering. Critics also worried that as the prison industry grew, more and more people would have a financial stake in keeping the prisons full, whether that happened through longer sentences or stricter sentencing.

In the 1980s, the management of adult prisons started to be transferred from governments to corporations. Firms that managed prisons were typically paid a per diem per inmate by the government. The lower the corporation could spend in daily costs per inmate, the higher the profits, which weren't inconsequential. Total revenues for private correctional services were estimated at $1 billion in 2001, and of 184 privately-operated prisons and jails around the world, 158 were in the United States, mostly in Texas and California.[20]

Did private prisons deliver on what they promised? A report compiled for the U.S. Bureau of Justice Assistance said no; private prisons proved no more efficient or safe than publicly managed ones. The 20 percent promised cost-savings turned out to be worth about 1 percent on average — realized mostly from lower labor costs since private prisons tend to hire non-unionized staff and fewer of them, then save money by paying lower wages and offering fewer benefits.[21] Still, according to the economic story, transferring the management of prisons to corporations is worth doing. And the story says the same thing is true of public libraries.

For many people, public libraries are iconic. Gary Paulsen, author of over 175 books, many for young adults, credited a public library with saving his life. As a teenager in northern Minnesota with an unhappy home life, he ducked into a small-town library one night to warm up. The librarian offered him a library card and kept feeding him books. Paulsen said, "It saved me, it really did. I still read like that, like I tell kids, like a wolf eats. I read myself to sleep every night. And I don't think any of the good things that have happened to me would have been possible without that librarian and libraries in general."[22] Legendary science-fiction author Isaac Asimov said, "I received the fundamentals of my education in school, but that was not enough. My real education, the superstructure, the details, the true architecture, I got out of the public library. For an impoverished child whose family could not afford to buy books, the library was the open door to wonder and achievement, and I can never be sufficiently grateful that I had the wit to charge through that door and make the most of it."[23]

Public libraries embodied something called library faith: the belief that books change lives. Library faith represented a foundational belief in "the virtue of the printed word, the reading of which is good in itself, and upon which many basic values in our civilization rest. When culture is in question," said political scientist Oliver Garceau, "the knowledge of books, the amount of reading, and the possession of a library — all become measures of value, not only of the individual but also of the community."[24] Public libraries also once shaped people's reading tastes, "improving" people through books. In the 1940s and 50s, librarians argued about whether or not "light" fiction should be allowed in the library because fiction was considered entertainment, something with little or no educational value, and libraries were supposed to be edifying.[25]

Libraries took it upon themselves to help people become informed and thoughtful citizens by keeping the knowledge and values needed for democratic society in circulation.[26] In 1852, the trustees of the Boston Public Library — the first library in America to be supported by public taxes — stated, "...it is of paramount importance that the means of general information should be so diffused that the largest possible number of persons should be induced to read and understand questions going down to the very foundations of social order, which are constantly presenting themselves, and which we, as people, are constantly required to decide, and do decide, whether ignorantly or wisely."[27] The United Nations called the public library "a living force for education, culture and information" and "an essential agent for the fostering of peace and spiritual welfare through the minds of men and women."[28]

In short, the public library didn't just contribute to the public good; it was the public good. We invested in it with our tax dollars because we believed our society was better off when our citizens were literate and educated. The library was the people's university, the great equalizer in society — the place where you could access books and learn for free regardless of your income.[29]

As a public good, libraries existed outside the boundaries of the market.[30] Libraries preserved the human record within the limits of their resources, protecting and transmitting that record for future generations.[31] They embodied intellectual freedom, the idea that you should be able to think and believe what you want. Because of that belief in intellectual freedom, diverse views — even those that were "unorthodox, unpopular, or considered dangerous by the majority" — were deemed to be in the public interest, and the library became a place where you could find alternative and competing points of view on a given issue.[32] In practice, intellectual freedom meant important but controversial books were put out on the shelf instead of banned or burned. Information about who was reading what was kept confidential, even from law enforcement, and everybody who used the library had equal access to the information they needed regardless of religion, ethnicity, gender, age, or economic status.[33] The library created information resources that the market wouldn't, because the private sector had no reason to invest in knowledge that didn't make money, and knowledge that is unorthodox, unpopular, or considered dangerous often isn't profitable.[34]

When the economic story spreads through your community and into the public library, library services become understood as a market, and what goes on in markets starts happening at the library. Information is transformed from a social good that helps to develop informed citizens into something to buy and sell and profit from. The library becomes an information business in the information services industry and starts to focus on what businesses focus on: customer service, cutting costs, efficiency, and productivity.

Librarians become information specialists who just happen to work in libraries. Chief Librarians become CEOs. Library patrons become customers, and libraries start gathering information about customer needs and wants through market research. Libraries become worth supporting not because they are a public good, but because they respond to customer needs.[35]

By 1980, public libraries were focused not on prescribing what patrons ought to read, but on being responsive to customers by giving them what they wanted.[36] What some customers wanted, of course, was to ban books, creating a conflict of interest between customer responsiveness and the library's historical dedication to intellectual freedom.[37]

As the economic story spreads into libraries, economic language spreads too. As one prominent librarian said, "Every time a dollar changes hands [at the library] there has been a business transaction. We establish a mission based on our values, we plan strategically and allocate resources accordingly, we engage competent and capable staff to make our products and services available, we monitor and adjust depending on our market's needs and desires. These are all business activities."[38] The profession started to ask itself, "What If You Ran Your Library Like a Bookstore?" and branch libraries in East London were renamed "Idea Stores."[39]

To be sure, many libraries embraced these shifts because of cuts in government funding. In 2010, American libraries from coast to coast — including the venerable Boston Public Library — again found themselves struggling to cope with city budget deficits in an attempt to avoid branch closures, staff layoffs, and reduced hours and services. In the past, as libraries struggled for shrinking government dollars, many had already adopted business strategies to address the shortfall. Libraries slowly became a place to make money, and a place for corporations to promote themselves and sell their products and services.[40]

When the library comes to think of itself as a business, it starts being discussed in terms of return on investment. The economic story says libraries should make money by developing their own revenue streams and opening bookshops, gift shops, and coffee shops. Libraries should also introduce user fees and charge for library cards. In the economic story, you are an individual, and as an individual, if you benefit from something like the public library personally, you should pay for that benefit personally. Though fees for library cards were controversial when they were first introduced because they flew in the face of the library principle of equal access to information, user fees now typically represent 10 to 15 percent of the average library budget.[41]

In the oil-rich Canadian province of Alberta, library user fees were introduced after government cutbacks in the 1980s. Even when the province became solvent and debt-free, posting multi-billion dollar surpluses and enjoying a reputation as the wealthiest province in Canada, the fees stayed. In the capital city of Edmonton, after user fees were introduced, library enrolment and circulation dropped significantly and had not recovered ten years later.[42] The smaller center of Banff, Alberta, chose to axe its library user fee; library membership soared 40 percent that year.[43] Although many libraries allow people to ask for the fee to be waived if it's unaffordable, as one librarian said, "[As] someone who grew up in a poor family, I feel that asking people for proof of their poverty humiliates them. (Surely being poor is humiliation enough without having to identify yourself as such to get 'special treatment' in what I feel is our most democratic institution — the public library.)"[44]

In the economic story, libraries are encouraged to raise funds by selling named space to individual or corporate donors. This was already happening in libraries to some extent; library buildings were being named after donors. The Carnegie libraries were named for steel magnate Andrew Carnegie, who financed more than 2,500 libraries around the world. What is different now, though, is that library parts are for sale.[45] Naming opportunities include the circulation desk, individual meeting rooms, study rooms, window reading nooks, reading benches, and the picture book collection. That kind of private sponsorship, though it brings in revenue, also creates a vicious cycle; companies get a tax write-off for their donations, which means less corporate tax ends up in city coffers. With less money available in public funds, libraries typically find themselves on the chopping block again, making them even more dependent on private sector funding.

In the economic story, the neutral public space that the public library once represented doesn't stay neutral. Prior to the Vancouver 2010 Olympics, public libraries in Vancouver were asked to make sure the brands of sponsoring corporations were given exclusive play at library functions. A leaked internal memo read, "Do not have Pepsi or Dairy Queen sponsor your event…Coke and McDonald's are the Olympic sponsors. If you are planning a kids' event and approaching sponsors, approach McDonald's and not another well-known fast-food outlet." Libraries were also advised to try to meet official sponsors' brand requirements. If only Sony equipment were available in the library, for example, instead of equipment made by official sponsor Panasonic? "I would get some tape and put it over the 'Sony,'" the Vancouver Public Library's manager of marketing and communications was quoted as saying, "Just a little piece of tape."[46]

The economic story interprets the "public" in public library in a new way. It says the management of public libraries ought to be outsourced to the private sector, which is more efficient and effective. Book-buying for the library is outsourced to corporations. Critics worry that outsourcing the development of the library collection is akin to corporations deciding which books are available to you in the library at all, and question whether books that challenge the status quo or that criticize business itself will find their way onto the shelves.[47] Even so, in 1997, the city of Riverside, California became the first documented library system to outsource the operation of its 25 library branches to a private company called Library Systems & Services, LCC (LSSI). Critics say the company runs libraries for less than cities can by hiring fewer trained librarians, and by paying lower salaries and offering fewer benefits to employees.[48] Yet by 2010, LSSI was America's fifth-largest library system, having "taken over public libraries in ailing cities in California, Oregon, Tennessee and Texas." In late 2010, LSSI won its first contract to run libraries in the financially-healthy city of Santa Clarita, California; the $4 million deal was described as "a chance for the company to demonstrate that a dose of private management can be good for communities, whatever their financial situation."[49]

After all, in the economic story, the public sector and the private sector are no longer distinct areas of activity that ought to be managed differently. In the economic story, the public sector and the private sector are the same sector: private.

6

YOUR PHYSICAL
AND SPIRITUAL HEALTH

To the extent that economic thinking is based on the market, it takes the sacredness out of life, because there can be nothing sacred in something that has a price. Not surprisingly, therefore, if economic thinking pervades the whole of society, even simply non-economic values like beauty, health, or cleanliness can survive only if they prove to be 'economic.'

—E.F. SCHUMACHER

You in the West have the spiritually poorest of the poor much more than you have the physically poor. Often among the rich are very spiritually poor people. I find it is easy to give a plate of rice to a hungry person, to furnish a bed to a person who has no bed, but to console or to remove the bitterness, anger, and loneliness that comes from being spiritually deprived, that takes a long time.

—MOTHER TERESA

FOR HUNDREDS OF YEARS, the human value at the center of medicine was health, says biomedical ethicist Daniel Callahan, "the integrated well-being of mind and body" — the healing of the sick, the compassionate relief of suffering. Doctors were expected to act in the best interests of their patients. Plato wrote, "The physician, as such, studies only the patient's interest, not his own…The business of the physician, in the strict sense, is not to make money for himself, but to exercise his power over the patient's body…All that he says and does will be said and done with a view to what is good and proper for the subject for whom he practices his art."[1]

Even so, doctors weren't always respected. In Roman times, doctors were decidedly low in status: they were slaves, freedmen, or foreigners. Until as late as 1745, surgeons were considered craftspeople who belonged to the same guild as barbers since both worked with their hands. A medical journal of the time remarked that when a promising young man chose to become a doctor, "the feeling among the majority of his cultivated friends is that he has thrown himself away."[2]

In the 1800s in England, doctors hovered around the edges of the gentry, trying to look and act like the upper class since professional success was about having the right aristocratic patrons and displaying the right social graces. In America, the aristocracy didn't exist, so medical schools and societies were launched, often by doctors themselves, to bolster the status of the profession. At the same time, legislation was enacted that controlled who could and couldn't open a medical practice.

As a result, in the 1800s, being a doctor was a hard way to make a living. Americans were wary of medical authority. Doctors didn't have stores of medical knowledge or techniques to pull from, and most families, isolated in rural areas with low incomes, could only afford to call a doctor if the situation was desperate. Doctors charged for mileage on top of the fee for a medical visit, and five to ten miles of travel meant the travel fee could be four or five times as high as the visitation fee. They ended up working long hours and traveling long distances to see patients. The image we still have today of the dedicated, selfless doctor comes from that era of medicine.[3]

During the Industrial Revolution, work that used to be done at home started moving into the factories, making it harder for family members to care for the sick at home. As steamboats and railways were built, cities began to develop. Better mobility meant that family members were more spread out than they had been, so they weren't always available to care for the sick. As cities grew, property values also started to rise, and many families could only afford to live in apartments, which left less space at home to care for the sick. More people were also living alone in cities, which meant the need for hospitals was growing along with the demand for doctors. At one time, few people used hospitals voluntarily because of the risk of infection; hospitals were more about charity than medical expertise and most were run by religious orders where nuns, doctors and nurses volunteered their time to care for the sick. You went to the hospital to die, or when you didn't have family or friends to care for you. If you were sick, you were simply safer at home.[4]

At the same time, doctors were also becoming more mobile. The invention of the telephone meant patients could call the doctor instead of sending for him, and the invention of the car meant doctors could reach patients faster; doctors were among the first car buyers. As doctors began to travel farther and faster, they saw more patients, increasing from an average of five to seven patients a day in the mid-1800s, to 18 to 22 patients a day by the early 1940s. As travel costs went down, medical care became more affordable. Doctors became more accessible, and people became more dependent on their services.[5]

Still, in 1900, medical practice was unsophisticated. New ideas were slow to be adopted. Most surgeons still used their bare hands when operating, and few pharmaceutical drugs existed. A medical education meant you'd sat through two years of mostly lectures at one of over 150 schools, many of which were for-profit and had low entrance standards.

Then medical knowledge started to grow. From the early 1900s to the early 1940s, x-rays, ECGs, and the four major blood groups were discovered, along with insulin, sulfa, penicillin and anaesthetics. Doctors became a symbol of healing. The growing demand for medical care meant that doctors could afford to give up lower-paying services and focus on higher-paying, more complex services that involved things like diagnostic labs, radiology, and surgical suites. Those complex services were often offered in hospitals now that medicine had advanced to the point where a doctor's expertise no longer fit into a black bag, and where the services offered were too expensive to be maintained in every doctor's office.[6]

As urbanization shifted care of the sick from families and neighbors to doctors and hospitals, health care became a commodity, something that was bought and sold. At the same time, though, medicine wasn't thought of as just another thing for sale. It was regulated because it dealt with serious issues like the relief of human suffering. Bad health care could have drastic consequences like disability or death, and most people who needed medical help weren't in a position to evaluate the kind of help they were getting.

The buying and selling of health care was also softened by the ideals that dominated the culture of the medical profession.[7] In 1934, the ethics code of the American Medical Association (AMA) said non-doctors (outside investors) profiting from medical work was "beneath the dignity of professional practice, is unfair competition within the profession at large, is harmful alike to the profession of medicine and the welfare of the people, and is against sound public policy."[8]

Before World War II then, medicine was a cottage industry financed mostly by wealthy patients and philanthropists. Not enough medical technology existed to support a health manufacturing industry, and the government was uninvolved in health care other than via licensing and tax laws. In 1946, most American citizens were uninsured and paid for medical services out of their own pocket, or sometimes paid in kind. But in 1946, medicine was also viewed as a profession, not a business. A patient's medical needs, by and large, were put ahead of a doctor's financial gain.

After the Second World War, funding that had gone to the atom bomb was redirected to medical research, and in the 1950s and '60s, major advances were made in surgery, radiation, chemotherapy, organ transplants, and tranquilizers. Medical knowledge had now grown too large for a single doctor to learn during training, and doctors increasingly began to specialize. In 1923, 11 percent of American doctors were specialists; in 1989, over 70 percent were. Specialists were paid more than generalists and enjoyed more prestige, but specialization also meant that a doctor's once-holistic view of you as a patient became fragmented, and personalized medical care started to fade.[9]

With the rise of new medical technology, along with specialization, insurance coverage, and unregulated payments for doctors' fees, medicine started looking attractive to outside investors. In the late 1960s and early 1970s, Wall Street started investing in for-profit health care facilities like investor-owned hospitals, nursing homes, home care, labs, and imaging services.[10] After an advertising ban in medicine was lifted, doctors and hospitals started advertising their services. Where open and public competition between doctors and hospitals had once been considered unethical and unprofessional, advertising now made that competition public, which strained collegiality.[11]

As investors started showing interest in health care, medical costs started to spiral due to inflation, growing research expenses, rising doctors' fees, higher hospital costs, more health benefits for employees, and an aging population (medical advances had lengthened our lives but now we faced the complications of chronic disease which we just hadn't survived to experience before). Malpractice suits were also rare until the twentieth century, when a growing number of lawsuits created "defensive medicine": doctors did everything they possibly could in a medical situation to avoid being sued for negligence.[12]

Technological advances in medicine were also proving expensive. Though new technology usually pays for itself because machines replace workers, in medicine that didn't happen. Instead, medical advances involving complicated equipment and procedures required additional experts to be trained in the technology and increased costs instead of decreasing them.[13]

The market was presented as a solution to all of these problems. The economic story says that a health care market will bail the government out of health care support it can no longer afford. Medicine started taking on the management practices of large businesses, and industrialization techniques were applied in the field. Private capital became a major player in the system, and much of the money was tied up in insurance companies and manufacturers of health technology. For-profit health services appeared in home care, kidney dialysis centers, care centers, and hospitals. Multinational health care companies grew and were said to be "to the old 'doctor's hospitals' what agribusiness is to the family farm."[14] An original $8 share in Humana, a multinational health care company, in 1968 was worth $336 by 1980; investments in hospital systems during those years returned almost 40 percent more in earnings than the average for other industries.[15]

In the early decades of the twenty-first century, health care is a multi-billion dollar industry. Medical schools now offer joint MD-MBA degrees and business school graduates hold top positions in medical organizations, even though as recently as 1978, doctors weren't expected to understand health care

financing and organization.[16] Managers of both not-for-profit
and for-profit hospitals, who earn salaries as hefty as those in
the private sector, are rewarded based on the net income of the
hospital, and hospital CEOs or presidents "are clearly accountable to their boards as business experts."[17] Health care policies
are laid out by business school professors and economists.[18]

Arnold Relman, former editor-in-chief of the *New England
Journal of Medicine* and the man who coined the term *medical-
industrial complex*, says the most important socioeconomic
change in a hundred years of American health care is the
movement from "a professional service for the sick and injured
into one of the country's largest industries" — a transformation of health care from the compassionate relief of suffering
to a profit-oriented business. Relman admits, "I am not saying
that business considerations were never a part of the medical
profession...or that physicians were in the past unconcerned
about their income...But the commitment to serve patients'
medical needs (as well as the needs of public health) and the
special nature of the relation between doctor and patient
placed a particularly heavy obligation on physicians that was
expected to supersede considerations of personal gain — and
usually did."[19]

Biomedical ethicist Callahan agrees. "[T]here is an
enormous difference," he says, "between a discipline and a profession whose practitioners do not resist the personal good life
when it comes their way, and one which has that life as its purpose."[20] Paul Starr, a Pulitzer Prize-winning sociologist adds,
"The contradiction between professionalism and the rule of
the market is long-standing and unavoidable. Medicine and

other professions have historically distinguished themselves from business and trade by claiming to be above the market and pure commercialism. In justifying the public's trust, professionals have set higher standards of conduct for themselves than the minimal rules governing the marketplace."[21]

Back in the 1960s, the norm as a doctor, according to the AMA, was to limit your professional income to "reasonable levels" because the "charging of an excessive fee is unethical... [the] fee should be commensurate with...the patient's ability to pay..."[22] Health care was considered to be about need, not someone's ability to pay, since health care dealt in quality of life as well as life itself.[23]

The economic story, on the other hand, says health care services are products, hospitals and doctors are sellers, and you as a patient, your government, and your insurance company are buyers. Your doctor is an entrepreneur competing with other doctors for your business. As a business, the health care industry promotes ever-changing products, "medicalizes" problems by advertising all kinds of conditions, stimulates interest in cures, builds consumer demand, and tries to get you out to the doctor more. Doctors can now be hired by insurers, which creates a conflict of interest between you and your doctor; an insurer typically wants to pay out as little as possible, so your doctor is caught in the middle, wanting to do what's medically necessary for you as a patient while being aware that his or her employer is eyeing the cost.[24]

In short, health care as a business is profoundly different from health care as a profession. Health care as a profession was founded on the relationship between you and your doctor; you trusted that your doctor was acting in your best interests.[25] But by the 1990s, that trust was starting to erode. In the United States, hospitals were commonly paid a lump sum per patient by insurance programs, and so could grow their profits by keeping their costs down; doctors could order fewer tests, hospital workers could be paid less, and patients who were critically ill could even be shipped to other hospitals, thereby creating a financial incentive for hospitals to treat the least sick and discharge them as fast as possible, keeping turnover high. Simply, it was more profitable to keep people out of the hospital than in. By 1997, over one-third of hospital revenues in America were realized from outpatient services.[26]

Conflicts of interest were also being pointed out in medical research. Before the economic story spread, research was supposed to be performed by disinterested parties according to the traditional norms of science. The *Journal of the American Medical Association* (*JAMA*), a leading publisher of medical research, saw its industry-financed research submissions drop 21 percent after it instituted a policy that required that data in company-sponsored medical trials be independently verified by university researchers. Still, since medical journals rely on corporate dollars (companies buy reprints of articles that support their products), *JAMA* "could face significant financial pressure to abandon the policy."[27] Another study released by *JAMA*'s editors found that in 2008, six of the top medical journals published a significant number of articles that were ghostwritten; other studies have shown that medical ghostwriters, whose work is hidden behind academic authors, are often sponsored by drug or medical device companies.[28]

That conflict of interest was also spreading to the medical classroom. In 2009, Harvard Medical School students questioned the influence of pharmaceutical companies in what was being taught, pressing for faculty to disclose their industry ties after pharmacology students discovered that a professor promoting cholesterol drugs and disparaging students' questions about side effects was a paid consultant to 10 drug companies, half of which produced cholesterol treatments. A then 24-year-old Harvard Medical student admitted, "We are really being indoctrinated into a field of medicine that is becoming more and more commercialized."[29]

A national survey of physicians published in the *New England Journal of Medicine* in 2007 found that 94 percent have "a relationship" with the pharmaceutical, medical device, or other related industries. That figure has contributed to concerns about how financial ties affect doctors' prescribing habits and has led to calls for transparency regarding the financial relationship between doctors and medical industries.[30]

As a consumer of medical services, in the economic story you are free to enter or exit the medical market as you please. You are, the story says, a knowledgeable buyer, and when the price of a health product or service gets too high, you are less likely to want to buy it. Most of us though, don't choose to be sick, and medical professionals say you are anything but knowledgeable because you don't have their extensive training. And if your life is at stake, chances are you will still buy whatever medical care you can get, no matter how much it costs; by 2007, over 60 percent of all U.S. bankruptcies were related to medical expenses.[31]

The economic story says that in the market, no one is dependent; as a buyer, you have a free choice of sellers, and as a seller, you have a free choice of buyers, so no unevenness in power is involved.[32] In reality, as a patient, you are heavily dependent on your doctor, and if you're sick, it's hard to "shop around" for a better deal like you're supposed to as a consumer. Finally, when the trust between you and your doctor begins to erode because you begin to suspect that your doctor, as an rational economic individual, is looking out for his or her own interests instead of yours, who is left to advocate for you in the health care system?

What do we gain in return for allowing the economic story in medicine and creating a medical marketplace, a health care industry? Do we enjoy better health or better health care? Relman doesn't think so. He points out that almost all of the reliable research points toward higher overhead and administrative costs in for-profit health care facilities than in not-for-profit facilities, and that the health service in those for-profit facilities is equal to that of non-profit facilities — or worse.[33]

Callahan points out that the market model of health care will never encourage us to use less medical care, will never put limits on our desire for ever better health, and will never limit the development and use of health care technology, no matter how expensive it becomes or how incremental the health gains might be. The economic story will never encourage us to accept our own inevitable aging and death. Instead, the economic story in medicine orients us away from all of that, keeps us struggling for ever-longer life through advances in medical technology that simultaneously produce billions of dollars for the medical industry.[34]

The economic story orients us not just physically, but spiritually, in matters of religious faith. Faith, said Wilfred Cantwell Smith, a scholar of comparative religions, is part of the human quest for transcendence. Faith is an orientation toward oneself, others, and the world, "a total response; a way of seeing whatever one sees and of handling whatever one handles; a capacity to live at more than a mundane level; to see, to feel, to act in terms of, a transcendent dimension."[35] Adhering to a certain religion is considered to be an expression of faith. In the United States, one of the most religious countries in the world, roughly 80 percent of Americans do just that, and identify themselves as Christians.[36]

Historically, Christianity is the dominant religion of the Western world. As a religion, Christianity encompasses specific beliefs and ideas. It's also an umbrella term that covers a variety of groups, some of which are convinced the others are misled at best and heretical at worst. Roughly 600 years after Christianity was made the official religion of Rome, the Christian church split into the Roman Catholic Church in the Western world and the Eastern Orthodox Church in the East. Then, during the Protestant Reformation, the Roman Catholic branch split again into Roman Catholicism and Protestantism. Across these centuries, says religious scholar Diana Butler

Bass, Christian beliefs and values changed with the times, in distinct historical periods.[37]

Early Christians, alive during 100 to 500 CE, thought of Christianity as a way of life, says Bass — not a sudden conversion or a doctrinal belief. Early Christians were generally pacifists; war involved killing, killing was murder, and murder was wrong, plus soldiers had to participate in acts of worship to the state, the gods, and the Roman emperor, which was considered idolatrous. These believers were warned against loving money, being stingy, and supporting the rich, and struggled with their relationship to material things like property and wealth. Justin Martyr, an early defender of the faith, said, "We who formerly...valued above all things the acquisition of wealth and possession, now bring what we have into a common stock."[38]

When Christianity became the official religion of the Roman Empire in 313, the church itself became rich and the biblical admonition to "go and sell what you have and give to the poor" became allegorical, not literal — a call to give up not money exactly, but whatever it was you happened to love more than God. From 500-1450, church and state joined together in the rise of Christendom. Money was poured into church art and architecture as a vision of God made manifest in the world; the stories of the Bible were represented visually in stained glass so pre-literate followers of the faith could "read" them. Islam emerged, and pacifism gave way to the crusades as Christians and Muslims warred for converts and territory.[39]

During the Reformation (1450-1650), art in Christianity gave way to words. Christianity changed from a way of life to a carefully worded confession of doctrine. Scripture was read for its transformative power. As a Reformation Christian, you lived the devout life in order to be saved. You believed you could be right with God by making society right, and social justice became a cornerstone of religious practice. Germany's Martin Luther called faith a gift and said God was about love, not judgment. France's John Calvin said Protestants ought to work hard and live frugally, that hard work was God's will and money amassed as a result was a sign of God's blessing.[40]

In modern Christianity (1650-1945), faith became tied to morality, not doctrine. Faith and learning became entangled. People valued certainty, believing that the truth could be searched out and solved. God could be accessed directly instead of experienced through church hierarchy, theology, or the written word. Religion was supposed to make people happy, and God's will could be reasoned out, replacing mystery with knowledge of nature's design. Progress was equated with hope, and people believed they didn't need to be transformed spiritually beyond where they naturally were.[41]

According to Bass, contemporary Christianity (1945-present), has grown more accepting of the traditions and practices of other religions, downplaying the divisions of economic status, class, health, education, and nationality to focus on practicing universal hospitality and justice.[42] In contemporary Christianity, people grow into the Christian life by becoming one of Christ's disciples, a spiritual apprentice formed in the image of God with habits and affections distinct from those of the world. Contemporary Christians aspire to care for the suffering, paying particular attention to the poor. They take

on the responsibility of caring for others because they consider themselves to be their brother's keeper based on the idea
that all human beings are children of God, brothers and sisters
created in God's image. Believing that people need God and
God's abundance, and that we belong to one another in communities, they trust our relationships with each other matter,
that our fates are intertwined.[43] In contemporary Christianity,
Christianity is formative, capable of making you a new person
in the image of Christ. Beliefs represent revealed truth, and
souls need to be redeemed from their original sinful state.

Then the story changed. Again.

The economic story says religion too can be understood in
terms of economic values and assumptions. Religious market
theory, in particular, says the world of religion is a religious
economy, and that the religious economy operates like a commercial economy. The religious market, like the actual market,
operates according to the laws of supply and demand. Your
interest in religion, as compared to your neighbor's, represents
variation in demand, and the different activities of different
churches represent variation in supply. People interested in
religion and spirituality are a market of current and potential customers. Different kinds of churches represent the set of
firms that want to serve those markets, and different religions
represent different product lines.[44]

In the economic story, you go to church as a buyer looking
to satisfy your religious preferences, whatever those preferences may be, since the content of those preferences doesn't
matter. No one religion is particularly "moral" or "good."

What is "moral" or "good" is just a consumer preference. There is no divine authority that makes your preference right or wrong; you are the sole authority on what you prefer, and in your spiritual search, you're searching for a religious product — a certain kind of religion — that meets your needs as a consumer.[45]

A church is an efficient and eager religious firm that exists to create, maintain, and supply religion to people like you. Because some people are more or less interested in religion than others, churches have to market their products vigorously and compete with other churches for your support. A single religious product line — any one religion — is inherently unable to satisfy the whole range of individual tastes because some people prefer their religion to be more strict or more permissive, more exclusive or more inclusive. Different segments of the market (children, teens, young families, empty-nesters, seniors, and shut-ins) will prefer different aspects of religion and so can be targeted with different product offerings as churches compete with each other for market share.[46]

In the economic story, America's most successful churches are deemed to be those that model themselves on businesses, complete with MBA-staffed management teams, strategic plans, identification of target markets, consulting services, and thousands of customers.[47] Pastors are CEOs. Laypeople are advised to "invest your life for the highest return" and live a life of "entrepreneurial faith" by applying the principles of business entrepreneurship to their spirituality: "When you are a spiritual entrepreneur, you are obeying God...According to

Scripture, being an entrepreneur is for everyone." Jesus is "the Ultimate Entrepreneur," having "set the standard for entrepreneurship...Jesus looked at life around Him and saw how He could add value."[48]

According to the economic story, Christianity is a brand and the cross, as a recognizable symbol, is Christianity's logo. Churches are to focus on efficiency, effectiveness, and organizational growth. As the former executive vice president and business manager of the Billy Graham Evangelistic Association put it, "Our job is to dispense the world's greatest product — with the greatest economy — to the greatest number of people — as fast as possible."[49] Churches grow by being responsive to customer needs, and customer needs are revealed through demographic and target market research that focuses on what the unchurched in the neighborhood want from a local church.

If you're already in the pew, you too belong to a target market. Your church is a social network and your pastor is a network connector who can spread product information and influence your purchasing behavior. In 2005, church leaders "had a chance to win a free trip to London and $1,000 in cash if they mentioned Disney's film 'The Chronicles of Narnia' in their sermons."[50] In Detroit, Chase Bank sponsored one megachurch's back-to-school festival by giving out free backpacks, and Pepsi donated a 15-passenger van to the church after the members bought 13,500 cases of product; the church's communications director described the deal as "win-win."[51] In 1998, Pope John Paul II's visit to Mexico City was sponsored by over two dozen corporations, and the Pope's image was used on packaging and billboard ads.[52]

In the economic story, there is no abundance of God — only scarcity. Relationships are impersonal and anonymous transactions in a religious marketplace. What you believe is a man-made product that needs to be marketed to appeal to people where they're at. Churches are religious service providers focused on customer service, organizational growth, and quantifiable success.[53] Theologian Darrell Guder writes, "It is now clear, as we look back over the last 100 to 125 years, that the value systems and operating structures of the large American corporation have become the dominant model for the institutional church. Over the last century, the Christian religion has become a big American business. We have centralized for efficiency and good management, developed major headquarters, accepted numerical and financial growth as the most important indications of success, introduced statistical measurement to determine that success, and made religion into a product."[54]

Finally, theologians Philip Kenneson and James Street warn that putting a marketing orientation at the center of the church's life "radically alters the shape and character of the Christian faith by redefining the character and mission of the church in terms of management exchanges between producers and consumers." They acknowledge that many things once deemed important in the Christian life do not fit in the management/marketing scheme of spirituality, and conclude that "not surprisingly, these matters are neglected in a marketing paradigm."[55]

7

YOUR EDUCATION

Just yesterday I was looking at the catalog of a nearby college. I couldn't believe the courses they were offering. How to use a computer. How to make a good investment. How to get a good job. How to, how to. There was hardly one course to make the inner man grow. If you suggest that a course in ancient history may play a role in a person's growth, they laugh at you. What relevance does it have to our life today?

—93-YEAR-OLD SOPHIE MUMFORD IN 1995,
INTERVIEWED BY STUDS TERKEL

We have taken the great leap forward and said, 'Let's pretend we're a corporation.'

—JOHN LOMBARDI, PRESIDENT,
UNIVERSITY OF FLORIDA, 1997

EDUCATION WAS ONCE THOUGHT of as a service to humanity, as a cornerstone of democracy. Through education, you came to an enlightened understanding of the world, became someone who could think critically, someone who knew how to participate effectively in society and how to hold democratic leaders accountable. Education was a public good, a social investment in our life together as a society. We believed that education improved us collectively whether we were personally the ones being educated or not. We used education to redistribute opportunity. Education would narrow the gap between the haves and have-nots by making access to a better life more equal. If you started out at a disadvantage, through education you'd have a chance to improve your life.

For the most part, education was kept in the hands of public institutions. We worried corporations might be tempted to exploit students who would find it hard to gauge the quality of education they were getting. Because we believed education was a public good, we subsidized it or paid for it in full with our taxes as a way to pursue social and economic goals deemed to be in the public interest.[1] Schools promoted a set of values that helped students understand what it meant to be a citizen. At school, you ideally learned to cooperate, resolve your differences, and work with people who were different than you. You learned that you might draw, write, run, or do math better or worse than the person next to you, but that there was generally a place for everyone. Each person had something to contribute.

Science was an important part of education, and had a lofty purpose: to create knowledge for the benefit of humanity. Science was a calling — not a career. Scientists didn't have to justify their work to outsiders because their research projects didn't cost much, and what those projects did cost wasn't paid for with public funds. A line, though not always a distinct one, existed between basic research that was primarily about discovering new knowledge for its own sake, and applied research where the real-world use of that knowledge was the focus.

As members of the scientific community, scientists were expected to share their data and results with other community members. Their research belonged to the intellectual commons. Publishing work in journals was about advancing scientific knowledge for the good of humanity, not staking a claim in intellectual property rights.[2] Bringing research to market wasn't that important, and the idea of personally profiting from your work was generally absurd. Getting something patented was a complicated process anyway. Scientists also worried that patents would erode the pursuit of basic research — and patenting something like medical research wasn't above-board because of the negative implications for public health. They conducted scientific research knowing their work was valuable and important because it benefited humanity.[3]

As a scientist, you were expected to stay detached and objective in regards to your research. You steered clear of emotional or financial entanglements in your work, seeking only the truth of the matter at hand and challenging the conventional wisdom in your discipline.[4] Truth in science mattered. Galileo had linked the two, saying: "The conclusions of natural science are true and necessary, and the judgment of man has nothing to do with them."[5] What he meant was that a scientific result was what it was — you couldn't just *create* a different outcome because you didn't like what you'd found. Galileo knew what he was talking about; he was tried for heresy and sentenced to house arrest by the Roman Catholic Church after he contradicted the church's teaching and claimed that the earth wasn't at the center of the universe.

For hundreds of years, science was "the pursuit of the Good and the True" — something that was intrinsically valuable because truth itself was intrinsically valuable. A scientist was viewed as a certain kind of person: someone who had the moral calibre to work without the rewards of wealth and power, to share his or her work with colleagues, and to stick to rigorous standards "in the service of a noble end: namely, the advance of knowledge and power on behalf of humanity."[6]

Then the story of education and science changed.

In the economic story, education is ushered into the world of markets and becomes a commodity. Students become buyers. Schools become sellers, service providers competing for business in the education services industry.[7] The economic story says that education is a private good, not a public one. Education is something that helps you get ahead in life as an individual. Education matters, not because it will help you become a fully formed and informed citizen capable of participating effectively in society, but because it will help you get a better job, make more money, and improve your quality of life.

Education becomes a financial investment that can offer you a high rate of return. You're to think hard about those rates of return when you choose what you want to be when you grow up. You're helped out by news headlines like this one: "Arts degrees reduce earnings."[8] In 2003, the BBC reported that university graduates with arts degrees in subjects like history and English make between 2 and 10 percent less than high school graduates. Language and education aren't lucrative, but law, medicine, math and engineering are solid financial investments. One of the researchers interviewed warned, "Feeling warm about literature doesn't pay the rent. Maybe an average arts student knows he or she is not going to do very well.

Maybe they do not. Education is a risk individuals take. We need to make sure people have the correct perceptions."[9]

The economic story tells us that because education is a private good and not a public one, the people who are getting educated should pay for that education themselves. Public funding for education drops. Tuition rates rise.[10] If you're enrolled in a professional program like law, medicine, or business that offers a high rate of return on your investment by giving you a chance to make a hefty future salary, you are expected to pay more for those higher returns. Between 1995 and 2002, tuition fees in Canada soared by 132 percent in medicine, 168 percent in dentistry, and 61 percent in law, compared to only 34 percent in all undergraduate programs — and after accounting for inflation.[11]

If you're not already wealthy, climbing tuition rates make it harder for you to become educated at all. In the economic story, though, access to higher education is not about keeping tuition rates down — it's about loaning students the money to pay for higher tuition, giving them better access to debt. More students are made eligible for student loans, and the amount students are allowed to borrow increases.[12] Those leery about taking on that kind of debt have fewer options than they once did. Scholarships and grants — money that doesn't have to be paid back — are now based more on merit than financial need, and the criteria used to measure merit are highly correlated with socioeconomic status. In other words, students who are more affluent to begin with have higher merit scores, which makes them more likely to be awarded financial aid that doesn't have be paid back. Education scholars observe that in the twenty-first century, more economic and racial inequality now exists in access to higher education than since the 1960s.[13]

The economic story says you should choose which school to attend based not on the quality of the teaching but on the brand recognition and cachet of the school and its degrees; a better brand represents a better return on your investment.[14] In your classes, you compete against other students to get ahead. You're ranked against your classmates and your ranking is largely based on how you perform as an individual.[15] If you're independent, flexible, adaptive, fast, self-governing, and entrepreneurial, you're someone to watch. High-performing, valued students are those who can help the school achieve its benchmarks in its own competition with other schools. If you're not a high performer, you're at risk of holding the school back and becoming labelled as an undesirable.[16]

How you perform matters, because in the economic story, your school educates you to give the country a competitive advantage in a global knowledge economy. Your school exists not to help you become an informed citizen, but to help the nation advance economically and competitively, to increase innovation that leads to economic development, and to train workers for the workforce.[17]

As a result, your school needs to be more entrepreneur-ial, driven to it in part since government funding is drying up anyway. Your school is to be on the lookout for new revenue streams; it's now buying and selling real estate, developing and selling retirement communities on campus, partnering with corporations and venture capitalists, commercializing intellectual property, starting businesses, and aggressively recruiting international students who pay much higher fees than you do for the same seat in the classroom. Your classes are also starting to be evaluated in terms of how cost-effective, efficient, and marketable they are.[18]

According to the economic story, schools should cut costs by outsourcing tasks and using private contractors instead of university staff to provide food, janitorial, laundry, and bookstore services. Schools should be less tied to their employees.[19] Tenured and tenure-track faculty positions — the kind of secure job professors used to get — are dwindling, falling from a combined 56 percent in 1975 to 35 percent in 2003.[20] Many instructors, often with PhDs, are now hired to teach on a contract basis for little money, few benefits, and no job security.[21] Marc Bousquet, author of *How the University Works: Higher Education and the Low-Wage Nation*, reported that a survey of the academic workforce shows that "fewer than one-third of the responding programs paid first-year writing instructors more than $2,500 a class; nearly half (47.6 percent) paid these instructors less than $2,000 per class…At that rate, teaching a full-time load of eight classes nets less than $16,000 annually and includes no benefits."[22] Meanwhile, behind the scenes, universities are starting to speak a new language of strategic planning, mission statements, cost-efficiency, excellence, performance appraisal, audits, cost centers, competition, choice, and accountability.[23]

In the economic story, science changes along with education. After science lost its moral high ground by creating the atomic bomb that was dropped on Hiroshima in the Second World War, science slowly became more industrialized. The economic story says that scientists ought to be scientific entrepreneurs — people who create knowledge *and* find a market application for it.[24] Research that requires significant outside funding becomes common, and scientists slowly become more dependent on winning grants and paying attention to funders' interests. Being able to win research contracts from outside the university becomes paramount. More and more research is published, but more of it is also criticized for being shoddy; solid scientific results require slow, painstaking work, but journals demand continual content and scientists need publication credits to improve their chances of promotion and tenure.[25]

The economic story tells us that scientific research, once part of the intellectual commons, is now intellectual private property. Former colleagues become competitors. Scientists move from freely sharing their data and results with the scientific community to forming, protecting, and monetizing their results through patents, licences, and partnerships with industry to protect future windfalls in case their findings can be commercialized successfully.[26] Knowledge commercialization centers appear on campuses and scholars are advised to think twice before discussing their work with colleagues, presenting research at conferences, or publishing their findings in order to protect their market opportunities. After all, research can generate major income. In 2000, licensing revenues for research results like the hepatitis B vaccine, the cancer drug Taxol, the sports drink Gatorade, and vitamin D technologies topped

$1.7 billion; revenues are typically split in thirds between the researcher, his or her department, and the university.[27]

In the economic story, scientists increasingly have financial interests in their own research results. Areas of the university that attract outside money, like business schools and chemistry and biology departments, become more respected than areas that don't, like the humanities. In 1976, a newly hired assistant professor teaching literature in the United States earned $3,000 less than a new assistant professor in business, but 20 years later, that gap had stretched to over $25,000.[28] Humanities advocates who once argued that studying ethics, aesthetics, language, history, religion, and the arts mattered because it was part of what it meant to be human now argue that the humanities matter because they contribute to economic development, or that the humanities literally are profitable because they generate more student revenues than expenses, compared to the physical sciences.[29]

In 1955, educator John Mursell warned that schools of a democratic society that failed to support and extend that democracy were socially useless at best or socially dangerous at worst. At best, Mursell said, schools would end up educating people who would go and earn their living indifferent to the obligations of citizenship, and at worst, schools would end up educating people to be "enemies of democracy — people who will fall prey to demagogues, and who back movements and rally round leaders hostile to the democratic way of life."[30]

Shortly before renowned anthropologist Clifford Geertz died at the age of 80, he wrote, "...aging scholars, like aging parents and retired athletes, tend to see the present as the past devitalized, all loss and faithlessness and falling away. But there does seem to be a fair amount of malaise about, a sense that things are tight and growing tighter, an academic underclass is forming, and it is probably not altogether wise just now to take unnecessary chances, strike new directions, or offend the powers. Tenure is harder to get…and the process has become so extended as to exhaust the energies and dampen the ambitions of those caught up in it. Teaching loads are heavier; students are less well prepared; administrators, imagining themselves CEOs, are absorbed with efficiency and the bottom line. Scholarship is thinned and merchandised, and flung into hyperspace. As I say, I do not know how much of this is accurate, or, to the degree that it is accurate, how much it represents but a passing condition, soon to right itself; how much an inevitable retrenchment from an abnormal, unsustainable high, the smoothing of a blip; how much a sea-change, an alteration, rich and strange, in the structure of chances and possibilities. All I know is that, up until just a few years ago, I blithely, and perhaps a bit fatuously, used to tell students and younger colleagues who asked how to get ahead in our odd occupation that they should stay loose, take risks, resist the cleared path, avoid careerism, go their own way, and that if they did so, if they kept at it and remained alert, optimistic, loyal to the truth, my experience was that they could get away with murder, could do as they wish, have a valuable life, and nonetheless prosper. I don't do that anymore."[31]

8

YOUR CREATIVITY

When you look back on a lifetime and think of what has been given to the world by your presence, your fugitive presence, inevitably you think of your art, whatever it may be, as the gift you have made to the world in acknowledgement of the gift you have been given, which is the life itself.

—STANLEY KUNITZ

Beethoven and Michelangelo, who sold their artworks for a profit, were entrepreneurs and capitalists.

—TYLER COWEN

IN THE ANCIENT WORLD, art was a skill — any human skill at all. Whether you made soup, painted, sculpted, or built chairs, what you made counted as art. You were a maker, someone who modified what was already there, unlike God, a creator who made something out of nothing. Art served a purpose; it didn't exist for its own sake. It was part of everyday life and was used to decorate functional objects like jars, furniture, and walls — so much so that if you were an artist, you were considered a manual laborer because you worked with your hands.[1]

In the eighteenth century in Europe, that holistic idea of art split in two. Artists became thought of as people who practiced the fine arts, including poetry, painting, sculpture, and architecture. Artisans, on the other hand, practiced crafts like shoemaking, embroidery, storytelling, or making popular music. By the end of the eighteenth century, artisans were thought of as entertainers or makers of useful things. But fine artists were considered to be God-like creators — people who embodied the power of nature itself, wrapped up in genius and inspiration. Their work didn't have to be functional; it was deemed worthy of contemplation in and of itself. Over time, the *fine* in fine art became so taken for granted that it disappeared for the most part, and art became its own realm of truth, spirit, and creativity.[2]

Toward the end of the eighteenth century, the patronage system that had seen artists sponsored by aristocrats who commissioned their work started to collapse during the French Revolution. Artists began to claim the freedom to do what they wanted to since they didn't have to follow their patrons' dictates anymore. That freedom meant artists became more dependent on selling their art to make a living since the legacy of the French Revolution meant art was no longer needed to adorn cathedrals, palaces, monuments, or tombs. At the same time, aristocrats, trying to raise money to flee the country, were selling off their art too, so the art market was flooded. That confluence of events gave rise to our image of the starving artist.[3]

By the end of the eighteenth century, people began to feel that art represented a deep and unknowable reality, that it revealed the truth and healed the soul. The word *romantic* was used to describe that feeling. Art became an exploration of truth, a way to recover ideals that had been dirtied by the greed and materialism of the Industrial Revolution. Art, in other words, was set up in opposition to commerce and became one of our highest values, something spiritual, transcendent, and redemptive.

Being an artist became understood as a spiritual calling, a vocation that demanded personal sacrifice and suffering. If you were an artist, you were graceful and imaginative, set apart, original, rebellious, and nonconformist. This Romantic idea of art was still evident in 1945, when economist John Maynard Keynes, then chair of the Arts Council of Great Britain, said the work of the artist was "individual and free, undisciplined, unregimented, uncontrolled. The artist walks where the breath of the spirit blows him. He cannot be told his direction; he does not know it himself. But he leads the rest of us into fresh pastures and teaches us to love and enjoy what we often begin by rejecting, enlarging our sensibility and purifying our instincts."[4]

Despite the spiritual nature of art and its opposition to commerce, artists had to strike an uneasy truce with the market. Your ability to survive as an artist, after all, hinged on being able to sell your art to the public. The muddle was that as an artistic genius and prophet, you were supposed to be free from the constraints of the market and the pursuit of market success, both of which were considered a threat to your artistic genius.[5] Artists even looked down on other artists who had popular success, because the public was assumed to be hostile to art and artists were supposed to suffer.[6]

Eventually, some of this art made its way into art museums. A museum, a "temple of the muses," is a place for us to preserve and pass on our human heritage based on the idea that the visual arts are a fundamental part of our common experience.[7] Stephen Weil, one of the leading commentators on museums, said art museums represent "a basic, irreducible commitment to the importance and vitality of works of art, to the excitement of their creation, and to the experience of seeing them… places where there is a stubborn insistence on the importance of the visual arts as a human activity…places, in short, where we celebrate the discoveries, delights, and deep awareness that can come uniquely through the visual."[8] Weil believed that art museums enrich our lives by teaching us how to look and how to see. He said, "To see well is to live richly, and the museum can be a school for seeing, a place where seeing is celebrated."[9] Art museums sharpen our perceptions, improve our visual intelligence, and widen our perspectives, Weil said, helping us make informed judgements about the past and more insightful choices about the future.[10]

The public was introduced to art museums in London, Paris, Munich, Vienna, and Rome in the 1700s. In America, early art museums were open to the public but were privately funded, often from huge personal fortunes. Private citizens started museums like the Boston Museum of Fine Arts out of civic pride, partly because the Puritan ethic stressed "the right use of riches," which led to a considerable amount of philanthropy, and partly because wealthy citizens willed their collections to museums since estate tax had made it too expensive to pass the collection on to heirs. But in 1913, federal personal income tax was introduced, and much of the money that had funded museums was siphoned away to the government instead.[11]

Since the government had effectively drained money from the arts with tax legislation, some citizens thought government should support the arts. With government support, museums would be able to subsidize admissions or allow free admissions altogether, improving public access. Government cultural policy in the arts came to be based on a Romantic ideal that the arts mattered and deserved public funds because art had a civilizing influence on us and contributed to our humanity. President John F. Kennedy said, "The life of the arts, far from being an interruption, a distraction in the life of a nation, is very close to the center of a nation's purpose, and is a test of the quality of a nation's civilization."[12]

The world of the arts was based on the idea that some forms of cultural and creative expression are better than others. The difference between high art and low art, says philosopher and visual art scholar Larry Shiner, was thought of as the difference between fine art and mass art, complex and simple, original and formulaic, critical and conformist, challenging and escapist, and (often) a small audience versus a large audience — the difference, some would say, between literary fiction and detective novels, or opera and pop music.[13]

Your role as the art-viewing public was to enjoy the art. If you didn't enjoy it, you obviously needed more encouragement and art education; the problem was *you*, not the art, because the focus of attention was on the artist, not the viewer. People generally assumed that the public's taste in art needed to be shaped and developed, and that's what museums were for. Giving you what you wanted to see was just not what an art museum was about. Weil said, "If a million people a month would pay three dollars to see, for example, a Matisse exhibition, we would not need financial support. And if we deliberately set out to find out what a million people a month *would* pay three dollars to see, then we would not be museums anymore — we would be Disneyland."[14]

Then the story changed.

After a change in tax rules in the 1970s, American corporations started giving more money to the arts.[15] Corporate patronage of the arts was geared toward certain kinds of programs, and that uneasy tension between art and commerce surfaced again. One policy analyst noted, "The only reason [corporations] have any interest in the arts, or at least the primary reason they have an interest in the arts, is one of visibility and public relations. And the minute you're talking about that, then you seem to be denying the main tenet for the arts, which seems to be an exploration or a discussion or a forum about the society in which the arts are existing. And when the arts are doing that in any kind of critical level or base, they are going to make waves, then they're going to make problems for the funders."[16]

Those problems didn't exist for long. In the economic story, cultural institutions like museums, which were once buffered from the market, are reclassified as creative industries within the world of markets. The creative industries, according to the

Hong Kong Centre for Cultural Policy Research, are "a group of economic activities that exploit and deploy creativity, skill and intellectual property to produce and distribute products and services of social and cultural meaning — a production system through which the potentials of wealth generation and job creation are realized."[17] These industries — also known as the cultural industries or the creative economy — are one of the fastest growing economic sectors, and include arts and crafts, fashion, film, theatre, the performing arts, advertising, architecture, publishing, music, and broadcast media.[18] The global worth of the creative industries ballooned from US$831 billion in 2000 to US$1.3 trillion in 2005, and the sector is now seen as central to the economies of Australia, Hong Kong, Singapore, New Zealand, the U.S., and the UK.[19]

In the creative industries, culture gets reinterpreted as a means of economic development. Culture becomes a lifestyle, a consumer choice. Art matters not because it elevates the human experience, but because it contributes to "international competitiveness, economic modernization, urban regeneration, economic diversification, national prestige, [and] economic development" — the way theatre in New York creates jobs and gets tourists to spend money on restaurants, hotels, and cabs.[20] Radiohead guitarist Ed O'Brien warned that the climate of the music industry has changed since the band was signed to a record label in 1991; creativity is now second to monetary concerns. O'Brien said, "[The industry has] become dominated by money...And I think the problem with that is that the creativity's gone out of the industry, the fun...

You realise there's something hugely missing now…the money men are now running the companies, whereas traditionally it's always been the creatives."[21]

As arts organizations become part of the world of markets instead of being buffered from it, their focus shifts from preserving human heritage and culture to attracting and building a paying audience. It's easier, after all, to measure artistic success in terms of tickets sold than in terms of something vague like aesthetic triumph. Arts organizations start to think and act like businesses, adopting management philosophies and marketing techniques and training staff in management and business practices. That training is offered mostly through business schools, which also stress the importance of the market.[22]

Museums start to see themselves as competing with all kinds of other organizations — like shopping malls — for your dollar of disposable income.[23] You're more likely to be part of a museum's target audience if you're a well-educated, upper-income professional, because you have enough disposable income to afford high ticket prices for cultural events, even though targeting the wealthy flies in the face of the old ideal of art for all, public accessibility, and art for education.[24]

In the economic story, museums develop closer relationships with corporations. In 2009, museums were reported to be accepting loans of ready-made art exhibitions that could be shown to the public for a nominal fee from companies like JPMorgan Chase, Deutsche Bank, and UBS.[25] Banks, in some cases, have collected art for up to 50 years, growing their collections by acquiring companies that themselves have art collections. Reports put the Bank of America art collection at 60,000 pieces; Deutsche Bank's collection is roughly 56,000 pieces. Museums like the idea of "renting" a turnkey exhibition because it's cheaper than to mount one themselves, especially in an economic downturn. Critics say the arrangement makes the company, not the museum, the curator of the exhibition, and that exhibiting a corporate collection in a museum increases the legitimacy and value of a collection that could one day be for sale in the market.

As those partnerships develop, museums begin to accept more explicit product tie-ins in their exhibitions. The Children's Museum of Indianapolis — the world's largest children's museum — teamed with Proctor & Gamble to name Swiffer its "official cleaner." The museum's press release read, "Swiffer products will be used throughout the 479,000 square-foot museum to try and lock dust and dirt in every exhibit it houses, including its most complex, 'Fireworks of Glass'...created by world-renowned artist Dale Chihuly. 'Dale Chihuly's artwork is one of the centrepieces of our Museum, and the preferred dusting solution to help keep it clean and dust-free is Swiffer...,' said Jeff Patchen, president and CEO of The Children's Museum of Indianapolis. 'After seeing how well it works on such a delicate piece of art as Chihuly's piece, we wanted to deepen our partnership with Swiffer to help keep our exhibits clean and dust-free for our young visitors to enjoy.'"[26]

The same museum also mounted a *Barbie™: The Fashion Experience* exhibit with the help of Mattel, Inc. In the museum's press release, the Senior Vice President of Marketing was quoted as saying, "For five decades, Barbie has been a symbol of fashion, cultural relevance and aspiration... we are thrilled to bring the brand to The Children's Museum...This one-of-a-kind interactive fashion and design exhibit allows Barbie fans to engage and experience the brand like never before."[27]

In the economic story, the artist moves from being considered a genius and prophet to being a small cog in the creative economy.[28] Creative thinking becomes a "prized, profit-producing possession" for individuals, corporations, and countries.[29]

Artists become art entrepreneurs, and success as an artist starts to be defined by how well one's art performs in the market. Artists were once supposed to look like they were above the market — driven to make art because they had to and not because they were trying to please buyers. Those who obviously catered to the market were thought to have compromised their artistic integrity; established British novelist Fay Weldon was criticized for promoting the products of Italian jewelry company Bulgari at least a dozen times in her novel, *The Bulgari Collection*, in return for payment.[30]

But in the economic story, successful artists aren't above the market — they're entrepreneurs and global celebrity brands whose art sells for millions. American artist Jeff Koons, known for his balloon animal sculptures exhibited around the world, is considered the successor of pop art icon Andy Warhol. Koons is said to view art in a capitalist culture as an inevitable commodity; he has industrialized his artistic process and employs over 120 people in West Chelsea, New York, to produce art that bears his name.[31]

He's not the only one. Englishman Damien Hirst, considered to be one of the most marketing-savvy artists in the world, is known for work like *The Physical Impossibility of Death in the Mind of Someone Living* — a 14-foot tiger shark preserved in formaldehyde, which sold for a reported $12 million.[32] Hirst said, "Money complicates everything. I have a genuine belief that art is a more powerful currency than money — that's the romantic feeling that an artist has. But you start to have this sneaking feeling that money is more powerful."[33]

Japanese artist Takashi Murakami was commissioned by luxury-goods manufacturer Louis Vuitton to create manga- and anime-inspired art for use on the company's leather goods, rugs, and plush toys. Murakami, who runs an art-making company outside of Tokyo, then created a series of paintings that featured the Vuitton logo and included an operating Vuitton boutique in his show that sold goods specifically produced for his exhibition at the Los Angeles Museum of Contemporary Art. In an interview with contemporary art author Sarah Thornton, Vuitton's fashion director, Marc Jacobs, explained, "It's not a gift shop — it's more like performance art…Witnessing what goes on in the boutique in the context of an art exhibition is as much an artwork as the art that went into the bags." In other words, where art was once opposed to commerce, in the economic story, art *is* commerce — and commerce is art. For his part, Murakami said, "My concentration is how to survive long-term and how to join with the contemporary feeling. To focus on nothing besides profit is, by my values, evil. But I work by trial and error to be popular."[34]

Admittedly, catering to the public makes it harder for artists and organizations to create and exhibit art that will challenge people and make them uncomfortable. But in the economic story, art isn't meant to do that anyway. Arts organizations begin to focus not on the artist, but on what customers want or need. Cultural experiences become entertainment commodities that are exhibited based on their potential to make money.[35] Successful creativity becomes creativity that attracts a large paying audience. The focus in art shifts from the creator to the consumer. If you as the art-buying public don't like the art that's in front of you, that's the artist's fault, not yours; the artist should have created something more appealing. In the economic story, artistic success is measured not by some aesthetic standard that involves educating the audience in how to experience and understand art, and not in terms of a piece's contribution to the body of work that came before it, but only by the price the work receives in the market.

And that tentative line that once existed between art and commerce? In the economic story, that line is erased.

9

THE MONOCULTURE EFFECT

*Instead of striking out on my own, I had conformed to a way of life
and modes of thought that had often seemed alien. As a result, I
found myself in a wasteland, an inauthentic existence, in which I
struggled mightily but fruitlessly to do what I was told.*

—KAREN ARMSTRONG

NOW THAT WE'VE SEEN how the economic story has spread,
changing how we think about work, our relationships with
others and the natural world, our community, our physical and spiritual health, our education, and our creativity, it's
easy to understand how our non-economic stories become
smothered by the master story. A monoculture based on economic values and assumptions develops. As the years go by,
we scarcely remember any other way to think, any other way
to live. Other stories that represent other ways of thinking and
being are lost to one ultimate value: whatever is economic.

As the monoculture aligns our experiences and expectations
with the economic story, our life together becomes more at risk.
Just as biodiversity embodies many forms of life and signals
the health of our ecosystems, value diversity embodies many
ways of life and signals the health of our social systems. When
we lose value diversity, we lose our ability to express ourselves
outside of the economic realm. We lose the "languages" we

once spoke in distinct parts of our lives — the language of family and relationships, the language of the natural world, of art and spirituality, of health and education, of the public interest and the common good. We learn to substitute an economic language for all of it.

But language isn't neutral. As we've seen in the last six chapters, using an economic language to tell all of our stories ultimately changes the meaning of the stories themselves. As language structures our thoughts and our thoughts structure our behavior, the monoculture begins to change the decisions we make and how we live.

When the story of education no longer tells us what it means to belong in society, to be a citizen, or how to participate with others in our life together, democracy dwindles. When the story of the common good becomes a story of economic development, the shared good that exists apart from economic development becomes hard to talk about. When the story of religion becomes a story about religious consumption and growth in market share, spirituality that exists outside of a marketing mentality fades. When the story of the creative arts becomes a story about what is economically successful, giving your art time to mature and creating without an intense focus on the market becomes naïve. When the story of work is about securing a moneyed future, following your passion becomes old-fashioned and ridiculous. When the story of your relationships is about out-performing and out-achieving others for a place at the table, our shared humanity is denied and we lose a place in the world where our acceptance and belonging isn't based on performance.

As the monoculture grows, we also lose something beyond value diversity. We lose the creativity that exists beyond the market, outside the boundaries of the economic story. This kind of creativity isn't just represented by artistic creativity — it also represents scientific creativity, relational creativity, spiritual creativity, and so on — the creativity that we can embody in all the different parts of our lives.

Imagine two circles that overlap a bit. One circle represents your creativity, and the other represents the economic story's world of markets. The area where the circles overlap represents creativity that is financially successful in the world of markets. The economic story says the circles should overlap as much as possible — that creativity is about producing something someone will buy. In actuality, the circles never completely overlap, and in an economic monoculture, the creativity that exists independently of the market is never considered to be worth pursuing.

In an economic monoculture, playing with ideas or materials for the fun of it and taking creative risks in any sense becomes viewed as increasingly dangerous. The risk of inefficiency, waste and market failure — of playing in the creative area outside the overlap — becomes too much of a risk to take. Over time, what is deemed creative in every field comes to represent the overlap between the circles — the common denominator, something the largest possible audience can agree on and buy.

But history shows that significant creativity emerges out of a sense of play and often has no foreseeable market application. Richard Feynman, a renowned physicist, became a little disgusted by physics at one point in his career. He remembered that physics had once appealed to him because he had played with it, had done whatever interested and amused him regardless of whether or not what he was doing was even scientifically important. After realizing he was burned out, he decided to play with physics again for his own entertainment.

One day, Feynman was in the school cafeteria and saw someone fooling around, throwing a plate up in the air. He noticed that the plate wobbled on the way up, and that the school medallion marking the bottom of the plate was going around faster than the wobbling. He started figuring out equations of wobbles, for fun. A colleague acknowledged the equations were interesting but questioned their importance. Feynman snorted and said they were of no importance whatsoever, that he was working on them for the fun of it. Slowly, his enthusiasm for physics returned. He said, "It was easy to play with these things. It was like uncorking a bottle: Everything flowed out effortlessly. I almost tried to resist it! There was no importance to what I was doing, but ultimately there was. The diagrams and the whole business that I got the Nobel Prize for came from that piddling around with the wobbling plate."[1]

It is this creativity that exists for itself, on its own terms, that is at risk in a monoculture. If the link between a creative idea and market success isn't immediately obvious, as it very often isn't (J.K. Rowling's first *Harry Potter* novel was turned down by a dozen publishers), the monoculture rejects it. A kind of conformity takes over. A risk-averse, I'll-do-what-worked-before mentality, or I'd-better-not-try-that-at-all attitude develops. Consequently, it becomes difficult to develop or find support for a creative idea or expression that is interesting, beautiful or elegant, if it does not also look like it will succeed in the market.

The kind of creativity that emerges from working on what interests you personally, regardless of what anyone else thinks about it, also requires an independent spirit. Joseph Campbell believed that if you follow your bliss, "you put yourself on a kind of track that has been there all the while, waiting for you, and the life that you ought to be living is the one you are living…follow your bliss and don't be afraid," he said, "and doors will open where you didn't know they were going to be."[2]

But that independent spirit is hampered by the monoculture's demands for conformity. When you conform to the monoculture's version of who you are and what the world is like, you lose your freedom along with your ability to be truly innovative in terms of your own life. Being able to draw on many different stories, not just the economic one, allows you to creatively and authentically meet the challenges that face you in your life. The monoculture, determinedly single-minded, insists that economic values and assumptions can be used to solve your problems, whether those problems are spiritual, political, intellectual, or relational.

Those pressures to conform to the monoculture aren't new. They are remarkably similar, in fact, to the pressures experienced by those who lived under communist rule in the ideologically-rigid society of Czechoslovakia, as described by Václav Havel, playwright and first President of the democratic Czech Republic.

In a society grown rigid with ideology, Havel said, you come to accept that you should live according to that society's values and assumptions. If you were to refuse to conform, there could be trouble. You could be isolated, alienated, reproached for being idealistic, or scorned for not being a team player. You know what it is you are supposed to do, and you do it, not least to *show* that you're doing it. You go along to get along, he said, and so you confirm to others that certain things in fact must be done if you are to get along in life. If you fail to act as you're expected to, others will view your behavior as abnormal, think you arrogant for believing you're above the rules, or assume you've dropped out of society. The society grown rigid with ideology gives you and everyone else the illusion that the way things are is the way things are meant to be; the story you hear is natural. It has been told and retold for years. Everyone tells it.[3]

In truth, Havel said, that story is not natural; there is an enormous gap between its aims and the aims of life. Whereas life moves toward plurality and diversity and the fulfillment of its own freedom, the system demands conformity, uniformity, and discipline. The system, Havel said, "is a world of appearances trying to pass for reality." That world of appearances operates on a kind of automatic pilot, permeating and shaping the whole society. Though the world of appearances is partly stable, it's also unstable because it's built on appearances. Living within that world, you don't have to believe in it, but you have to *act* as if you do to get along in life.

Sometimes the whole thing seems innocuous enough for you to shrug and say, *What's wrong with going along with the world of appearances anyway?* You then accept the rules of the game, Havel said, become a player in the game, and so make the game possible in the first place. But that pattern of conformity also helps you hide from yourself that you are relating to the world through a rigid ideology, and the ideology creates the illusion that the way things are is a natural extension of the human order and the order of the universe. By accepting your life in the world of appearances, Havel said, you begin to "live within a lie." That eventually leads to a profound crisis of human identity: you're left with no sense of responsibility for anything more than your own survival in the system.[4]

If you try to live apart from that world of appearances, which Havel described as an attempt to live within the truth, "the bill is not long in coming," he said. You may lose your position and your promotion, your salary and vacation. Those around you will wonder about you, "not out of their own convictions, but because they want to avoid contamination by association..."[5]

The cost of living apart from the world of appearances is high because your act has repercussions far beyond the act itself. When you break the rules of the world of appearances, you show it is possible to live within the truth instead of living within the lie. Nonconformity must therefore be snuffed out.

An example may help make the point clear. In Australia, as around the world, the economic story has been adopted in universities, to the dismay of many scholars. Researchers studying the working lives of Australian academics encouraged those scholars to make peace with these profound changes. The authors warned that critique, which has traditionally been central to the role of the academic, was in this case not a way to conserve or increase capital "in a changed game," and that opposing the changes would have "little effect on how the game is played." They said, "Undoubtedly there will be people not playing but they won't be heard amongst the din…It is far more strategic to [compromise and] remain in the game" rather than "sideline themselves and their causes" and make themselves a target for those in power. [6]

One of the academics interviewed for the research said, "There was another guy who believed as I did over [an] issue… and in the end he resigned…But from his resignation I learnt that a stone can sink without a ripple. His letter of resignation never even made it to the table of the executive officer. And he disappeared without a trace. And that's the option people who wish to remain pure and take principled positions have: to disappear without a trace."

The researchers concluded that any discussion about the role of the market in higher education "needs to be clothed in the language of the market, language that has currency," saying, "a clever sailor can set the sails in such a way as to use the wind to travel in any direction he/she chooses…that is the possibility and the challenge [we] must now grasp: to set the sails so as to ride the winds of the market in ways that enhance the very best of [our] work and…life."[7]

Remember, the economic story says you are rational and will act in a way that maximizes your own best interests. As a rational individual, you will choose the course of action that allows you to reach your goals and *costs you the least of your resources to do it.* Because holding to your convictions can obviously *cost* you more than it would to say or do nothing (you too could sink without a ripple), in the economic story it is not in your best interests to hold to those convictions. Instead, it's in your best interests to keep your head down, to not draw attention to yourself, to not rock the boat.

At the same time, taking a principled stand at key points in our lives is one of the most human things we can do, one of the things our humanity asks of us now and again. So while the decision to count the cost and choose not to pay it is entirely rational and justifiable in light of economic values and assumptions, that rationality is not the whole story. Oscar Wilde put it this way: "The fatal errors of life are not due to man's being unreasonable: an unreasonable moment may be one's finest moment. They are due to man's being logical. There is a wide difference."[8]

Life, in other words, no matter how you live it, exacts a toll. Living beyond the economic story is costly, but living within the economic story and the monoculture just costs us in another way. When what we once valued intrinsically — truth, beauty, goodness, justice — becomes just another means to an economic end, and we accept life within the monoculture, we are deprived of our higher-level human needs. When our higher-level needs are denied, we develop what psychologist Abraham Maslow called *metapathologies*: "sicknesses of the soul."[9]

The choice isn't an easy one; how should we live? Do we conform to the monoculture and align ourselves with the economic story, or do we exile ourselves from the story that defines so much of our culture? Asked another way, if life is going to exact a toll no matter what you do, what's stopping you from living exactly as you please, telling your own stories, in line with your own deepest values?

10

FINDING ANOTHER WAY

Insight separated from practice remains ineffective.

—ERICH FROMM

THE TIME MAY COME when you find yourself drawn to move beyond the economic monoculture, its singular story, and its world of appearances. You may wake up one day, determined to live many stories, to live your life in a wider spectrum of human values instead of in a narrow channel of economic ones. Trying to move past that monoculture isn't about trying to fix the world for anyone else. You're simply trying to affirm your own identity, Václav Havel said, by rejecting what distances you from your own life. You're trying to live with dignity, free from manipulation. The question then arises: what does that kind of life look like?

A decision to transcend the monoculture isn't revealed by any one activity in particular. Havel pointed out that first attempts to move past the world of appearances might look like *not* doing certain things — not doing what others expect, not meeting certain demands. Instead, you gradually and quietly begin to live in a way that's aligned with your deepest values instead of with the limited values of the monoculture. You begin to be more intentional about your decisions and purposefully open yourself up to a wider range of values in different areas of life.

As you begin to live aligned with your deepest values instead of solely economic ones, your actions from day to day can in time give birth to something more articulate and structured, something Havel called "the independent spiritual, social, and political life of society."[1] That independent life isn't separate from the rest of life — it's simply marked by a high degree of inner freedom that comes from moving past the economic story and the monoculture. The independent life can take almost any form. You don't automatically have to quit everything you're doing and move to the country to transcend the monoculture. The independent life can encompass whatever it is you do, wherever you are, in whatever sphere of activity you already happen to be in.

As time goes on, that independent life naturally begins to be organized in one way or another, heralding the development of what Havel called parallel structures. Parallel structures, he said, are about the daily human struggle to live in freedom, truth and dignity — an articulated expression of living within the truth of life. Parallel structures give you room to live a different kind of life and grow from the needs of real people, bubbling up from below instead of being mandated from above, and developing organically.[2]

Parallel structures are not about dropping out of society or isolating yourself from the world. Instead, they invoke a sense of responsibility to and for the world, and so point to some-thing beyond themselves. They're open to everyone, available to all. They further free thought and alternative values and behavior. They do not represent a sure thing; you participate in them because you are compelled to, not because what you're part of stands a good chance of becoming a mass movement. The structures ultimately demonstrate, Havel said, "that living within the truth is a human and social alternative."[3]

Parallel structures are not counter-cultural structures; they are parallel precisely because they emerge *alongside* the mono-culture. Even as you engage with them, you are still connected to the monoculture's world of appearances in a thousand dif-ferent ways, through economic structures and value systems that already exist, and which you inevitably will continue to interact with in your daily life.

Nevertheless, there are concrete ways to begin to tran-scend the values and assumptions of the economic story that are embodied in the monoculture. Three such parallel struc-tures are the Slow Food movement, Christopher Alexander's pattern language, and Marshall Rosenberg's Nonviolent Communication.

Food is essential to life. According to the economic story, food represents a market. Buyers want to buy food that meets their needs and costs them the least of their resources. Sellers want to supply the best food they can for the lowest price possi-ble so they can sell more; the more productive and efficient they are, the higher their profits will be. The economic story says that when the market for food operates at peak efficiency, there's a balance between supply and demand; sellers won't produce what doesn't sell, and buyers won't pay for what they don't need. That kind of efficiency keeps everyone from wasting resources, which are scarce because there's never enough of anything to go around. Peak efficiency occurs when markets and market competition are as widespread as possible throughout the world.

Applied to food, the economic monoculture says we ought to be as efficient and productive as possible in how we grow and produce food, and as efficient and productive as possible in how we prepare and eat it. From a monoculture perspective, industrial agriculture makes sense. It's efficient. It allows us to mass-produce almost everything we eat — from chickens and eggs, to cows and pigs, to fish and vegetables, to corn and wheat. Through mass production, we achieve economies of scale that allow us to produce plenty of food for cheap prices. Tools and methods that allow us to increase food productivity, that lower prices and inconvenience for buyers, or that increase profits for sellers are positive from an economic perspective, whether those tools and methods include pesticide use, animal crowding in cages and pens, fish farming, genetic engineering, or seed patenting, because the economic story is a story about what is good for buyers and sellers — individuals, not group members, who are rational and who want to maximize their own self-interest. Economist E.F. Schumacher put it this way: "Call a thing immoral or ugly, soul-destroying or a degradation of man, a peril to the peace of the world or to the well-being of future generations; as long as you have not shown it to be 'uneconomic' you have not really questioned its right to exist, grow, and prosper."[4]

A parallel structure approach to food, on the other hand, is embodied in the Slow Food Movement. In Italy in the 1970s, a group of young political activists wanted to rediscover the pleasures of food, the sensual experience of producing, preparing, cooking, and eating it. The Slow Food movement was born, then launched internationally in Paris in 1989 when 250 delegates from Italy met to eat a meal together. The movement, in other words, bubbled up organically through the lives of members around the world.

Slow Food enthusiasts say that food isn't just necessary — it's enjoyable. Because food is woven throughout our lives, how we approach it is a sign of how we approach life itself. Slow Food, as a parallel structure, gives us room to live a different kind of life — a slower, more pleasure-filled life that has itself come to be known as slow living. Slow living is not a retreat from daily life; neither is it laziness nor a nostalgic return to the past. Instead, say scholars Wendy Parkins and Geoffrey Craig, "slow living is a process whereby everyday life — in all its pace and complexity, frisson and routine — is approached with care and attention…is above all an attempt to live in the present in a meaningful, sustainable, thoughtful and pleasurable way."[5] In that way, the Slow Food movement, as a parallel structure, serves the human struggle to live more freely and truthfully.

The development of the Slow Food movement has not been smooth or certain, as is true of parallel structures. Two early adherents and central figures in the movement, one Italian and one American, both had nearly ruinous experiences with money; Alice Waters, owner of Chez Panisse, almost lost her restaurant, and Carlo Petrini lost funds in an early project — but for both, says author Geoff Andrews, "money was secondary to their wider purpose and rarely got in the way of their latest ideas."[6]

The Slow Food movement is concerned for the environment of which it is a part, and values sustainability and the growth of food that is healthy for us and for the world. Because food and the environment are inextricably connected and food culture is linked to culture at large, the Slow Food movement, as a parallel structure, invokes a sense of responsibility to and for the world. The movement is also open to everybody, transcending political, economic, and cultural divides, and grows from the needs of real people. We all need to eat. Healthy food helps us thrive.

Breaking bread together around a table is also one of the great human traditions, one of our rituals for creating something that goes beyond physical sustenance. Eating together builds trust and friendship and gives us a chance to relax in each other's company. Jean Vanier, founder of the L'Arche communities for the developmentally disabled, said, "[Meals] are times for laughter, because laughter opens people up, and a group which laughs is a group which is relaxed. And when people are relaxed, they can begin to grow together."[7] The Slow Food movement encourages you to rediscover the pleasure and wisdom of food for yourself and for those you love, to relearn simplicity, fresh ingredients, quality, and the communal feel of your knees under the table with others. The Slow Food movement promotes taking that time to prepare food and eat together and so represents alternative values and behavior to those of the monoculture.

An economic approach to the built environment says buildings should be modular inside and out rather than organic to the land the building is on and the environment the building is in, because modular components are efficient and cost-effective. The values and assumptions of the economic story also have little regard for how the physical space that emerges as a result of the economic story impacts those who use the space day after day. In the economic story, what future buyers might think about our space matters at least as much as our own needs. We must appeal to the market, whether we are planning to sell our homes right away or not. As designer Ilse Crawford put it, "In creating our homes we have failed to pay attention to many of our true needs, the ones that really make a home warm and nurture those that live in it. At times, the whole language surrounding the home reeks simply of the balance sheet. Think of those terrible dinner parties where the talk is of the property ladder and good investments, and the TV programmes that show how to decorate in order not to put off potential purchasers."[8]

A parallel structure that exists alongside that economic approach to the built environment is the pattern language developed by architect Christopher Alexander. Alexander's two most influential books, *The Timeless Way of Building* and *A Pattern Language*, lay out the theory and instruction for a new language of building and planning. The language includes detailed patterns for how to build towns, neighborhoods, houses, rooms, and gardens that are not in the least modular, and so make us feel more alive, more ourselves. In his work, Alexander found that while people may differ on what they like about a physical space, they almost always agree about whether the space *feels* alive or not. That sense of aliveness is the fundamental feature that makes a structure live, though buildings take on a thousand faces across the centuries. He explains, "There is one timeless way of building. It is thousands of years old, and the same today as it has always been… It is not possible to make great buildings, or great towns, beautiful places, places where you feel yourself, places where you feel alive, except by following this way."[9]

Alexander's pattern language literally gives us room to live a different kind of life, as parallel structures do, because a pattern language helps us create living structures to inhabit. Alexander and his colleagues worked for eight years to identify the patterns based on people's feelings about what kind of space made them feel alive, more themselves. That means the patterns developed organically, as parallel structures do.

The patterns Alexander and his colleagues developed, all 253 of them, are connected. Each is linked to "larger" and "smaller" patterns above and below it, and to patterns of the "same size" around it. When you imagine or find yourself in a room that feels pleasant and comfortable, where you feel relaxed and most yourself, chances are at least some of the patterns are at work in that room. Given a choice, for example, people intuitively feel more comfortable in rooms where daylight enters on at least two sides, and tend to avoid rooms where daylight enters from one side only (the Light on Two Sides of Every Room pattern). The more conscious you are of the pattern language, the more you'll understand how to shape your space in a way that makes you feel most yourself and most at home.

The pattern language aims to put the needs of human beings at the center of architectural design. Alexander calls this a genetic approach to creating an environment that nurtures human life. Though he called his theory "a new attitude to architecture and planning," a pattern language isn't meant to prescribe a way of thought to anyone — it's meant to make you aware of your own pattern language and to improve it. The idea is that you know what you need from a physical space better than anyone else, even an architect, because you know your particular circumstances best. In public spaces, for example, we often wear paths in the grass cutting across from one point to another instead of staying on the sidewalks; the sidewalks are laid where builders wanted us to go, but the paths show how we actually use the space day after day.

A pattern language encourages you to think for yourself by telling you how the relationships between patterns of an environment work in an abstract way "so that you can solve the problem for yourself, in your own way, by adapting it to your preferences, and the local conditions at the place where you are making it."[10] In that way, a pattern language, as a parallel structure, involves free thought and alternative values and behavior. The language also explains why you feel more your-self in some places and less yourself in others, so you can make your own environment feel more alive.

Still, the success of the language hasn't been absolute. William Saunders, editor of *Harvard Design Magazine*, acknowledged that while Alexander's pattern language work has been immensely influential in the design world and in fields outside of architecture such as computer programming, "in the architecture schools I know," he said, "it is as if this book did not exist."[11] Alexander himself admits that over two billion buildings make up our built environment around the world today; most of those are not built according to a pat-tern language and so we experience them as dead space. He confessed, "When I started at twenty-five, thirty, years ago, I really thought that I would be able to influence the world very fast. Especially when I got to the pattern language. I thought, boy, I've really done it. This is going to work. No problem. The patterns are self-evident and true. They will spread. And, as a result, the world of buildings will get better. Hey presto. But it hasn't worked out like that. In practical terms I've done almost nothing…A few thousand buildings have been influenced… But meanwhile, we've still got this gigantic amount of con-struction out there which is defining the world that all of us live in, that is still going on, in exactly the same fashion."[12]

Nevertheless, the pattern language is powerful, a living lan-guage rooted in our very nature and behavior. The patterns grow from the authentic needs of real people because they combine to build structures that focus not just on aesthetics, but on what it feels like to live in a space day after day. Because we all exist in the world in a physical space of some kind, a pattern language is open to all of us and can be shared. We can each join in shaping our environment, Alexander says, because the power to create something alive and beautiful lies in each of us.

Because the pattern language teaches us how to create environments that make us feel more alive and more ourselves, it serves the human struggle to live more freely and truthfully. Alexander says, "It is a process which allows the life inside a person, or a family, or a town, to flourish, openly, in freedom..."[13] The root question, he points out, is under what circumstances is the environment good? Will this pattern make human life better? Will it make people more whole in themselves? A pattern language, he says, in its essence, is a fundamental worldview: "It says that when you build a thing you cannot merely build that thing in isolation, but must also repair the world around it, and within it, so that the larger world at that one place becomes more coherent, and more whole; and the thing which you make takes its place in the web of nature, as you make it."[14] In that way, a pattern language, as a parallel structure, invokes a sense of responsibility to and for the world, holding out an alternative to the monoculture.

An economic approach to relationships and human interaction says that your relationships are transactional. The economic monoculture says the world is made of markets, and people are buyers or sellers in those markets. Your relationships with others are arms-length and impersonal, and in those relationships you each try to maximize your own interests as rational individuals. You expect to have few obligations to each other (if any) outside of what's involved in the transaction at hand, and try to minimize your long-term commitments.

A parallel structure that exists alongside that monoculture approach to human interaction is Marshall Rosenberg's method of Nonviolent Communication. Nonviolent Communication is about communicating with people in a way that leads to better outcomes. It represents a way of speaking and listening that helps us exchange information and peacefully resolve our differences instead of defending ourselves, attacking others, or withdrawing when we are judged or criticized. It is a set of alternative behaviors based on values and assumptions that differ from our usual methods of communication.

Nonviolent Communication assumes that the most satisfying motivation you have for doing things is the enrichment of life, and that you can communicate from that basis instead of from fear, guilt, blame, or shame. The method values language that contributes to goodwill instead of to resentment or lowered self-esteem. It supports freedom of thought by encouraging you to take personal responsibility for your communication choices and for improving the quality of your relationships.

By focusing your attention on four components of the Nonviolent Communication process, you can learn to reframe how you express yourself and hear others.[15] You can move from responding to others automatically to responding consciously based on an increased awareness of what you're hearing and saying. In that way, Nonviolent Communication, as a parallel structure, creates space for you to live a different kind of life. Too, because we all communicate and have differences to resolve, Nonviolent Communication is open to everyone and grows from the needs of real people, as parallel structures do. It aims to "strengthen our ability to remain human, even under trying conditions."[16]

The method of Nonviolent Communication developed organically out of founder Marshall Rosenberg's own life experience. As a Jewish boy growing up in Detroit in the 1940s, Rosenberg was bullied and beaten up at school for being a "kike." Those experiences led him to ask what disconnects us from our compassionate nature, leading to violence, and what allows some of us to stay connected to that compassionate nature no matter what our circumstances. Rosenberg was struck by the central role words play in those experiences. In graduate school, he developed an approach to speaking and listening that helped people stay connected to compassion in their communication style. By 1984, he had founded the Center for Nonviolent Communication and was training people how to use the method to help prevent and resolve conflict.

As a method, Nonviolent Communication has, in some ways, been very successful. Many testify to how the communication style has changed their relationships, and the method has been used in conflict zones in Sierra Leone, Sri Lanka, Rwanda, Burundi, Bosnia and Serbia, Columbia, and the Middle East. Rosenberg himself tells how he had a chance to use Nonviolent Communication on the spot in a mosque at a refugee camp in Bethlehem while he was speaking to a crowd of about 170 Palestinian Moslem men. He recalls, "Attitudes toward Americans at that time were not favourable. As I was speaking, I suddenly noticed a wave of muffled commotion fluttering through the audience. 'They're whispering that you are American!' my translator alerted me, just as a gentleman in the audience leapt to his feet. Facing me squarely, he hollered at the top of his lungs, 'Murderer!' Immediately a dozen other voices joined him in chorus: 'Assassin!' 'Child-killer!' 'Murderer!' Using Nonviolent Communication, Rosenberg immediately and publicly started a dialogue with the man that lasted for over twenty minutes. Rosenberg said, "I received his words, not as attacks, but as gifts from a fellow human being willing to share his soul and deep vulnerabilities with me. Once the gentleman felt understood, he was able to hear me as I explained my purpose for being at the camp. An hour later, the same man who had called me a murderer was inviting me to his home for a Ramadan dinner."[17]

But despite the success of the method, conflict in communication obviously continues around the world, demonstrating that the success of a parallel structure does not lie in eradicating other structures completely, though reform is certainly possible. As a parallel structure, the method serves the human struggle to live more freely and truthfully, focusing on our shared values and needs. It invokes a sense of responsibility to and for the world by reminding us that how we communicate affects others, sending out ripples far beyond us for better or for worse, reminding us each day that we have another chance to communicate for the better. In that way, Nonviolent Communication exists alongside the transactional, impersonal, and short-term approach to communication represented by the economic monoculture, holding out a peaceful alternative based on compassion and a belief in the intrinsic merit of human beings.

These three examples of parallel structures — the Slow Food movement, Christopher Alexander's pattern language, and Marshall Rosenberg's Nonviolent Communication — speak to the power and presence of parallel structures in the world. But the visibility of these examples obscures the most important thing about them: the vibrant independent life of society that precedes parallel structures is the 90 percent of the iceberg that lies hidden in the water. That hidden independent life happens quietly all around us, day after day, as thousands of people struggle to live freely and truthfully in their own way, in their own lives.

A small, quiet decision to live within a wider spectrum of human values is easy to overlook and dismiss as unimportant, as negligible. It's easy to believe that unless a mass movement develops, nothing will ever change, that unless society wills something en masse, the world will go on as it always has. Albert Einstein observed that while we are what we are as human beings because of our membership in the human community, the valuable material, spiritual and moral achievements that we receive from society — paradigm-shifting achievements like the use of fire, the cultivation of edible plants, and the steam engine — are brought to us throughout the generations by creative *individuals*. "Only the individual can think," Einstein said, "and thereby create new values for society, nay, even set up new moral standards to which the life of the community conforms...The health of society thus depends quite as much on the independence of the individuals composing it as on their close social cohesion."[18] It's easy to believe that a quiet, obscure life that is little known and little seen makes little difference. But it is individuals living quiet lives who mobilize their inner resources to break with the social order. It is individuals living hidden lives who stand their ground and act. It is individuals living unseen lives who give birth to change, who risk retribution, who nurture independence.

That independent life begins with discovering what it means to live alongside the monoculture, given your particular circumstances, in your particular life and time, which will not be duplicated for anyone else. Out of your own struggle to live an independent life, a parallel structure may eventually be birthed. But the development and visibility of that parallel structure is not the goal — the goal is to live many stories, within a wider spectrum of human values.

That is what it looks like to live free from the economic monoculture's manipulation, to live the breadth and depth of all of our stories, to live with dignity.

EPILOGUE

Once we're thrown off our habitual paths, we think all is lost; but it's only here that the new and the good begins.

—LEO TOLSTOY

Go out in the woods, go out. If you don't go out in the woods, nothing will ever happen and your life will never begin.

—CLARISSA PINKOLA ESTÉS

STORIES TELL US WHO we are and what the world is like. When you hear one story often enough, you come to believe it's true. When that single story becomes our only story, a monoculture emerges. A monoculture changes everything, shaping how we think and how we live. It comes to seem like the only reasonable reality. Our other stories, the ones that told us what life was like beyond the monoculture's values and assumptions, that a kind of life even *exists* outside of its values and assumptions, fade. We come to believe that the economic story is the story of life itself, that being rational, efficient, productive and profitable are the ultimate expressions of being in the world.

As you now know, the economic story is changing how we think and act in terms of our work, our relationships with others and with the natural world, our community, our physical and spiritual health, our education, and our creativity. Now that you know what to look for, you'll see evidence of the monoculture and the economic story in the books and magazines you read, on television, at work, and in conversations you overhear and have yourself. The diversity of values and stories that once sustained us in different parts of life are giving way. That loss puts us at risk. Once you lose the diversity of stories that sustained you in different parts of your life, shaping who you are and how you live, it's hard to even think beyond the economic story, harder still to recognize how a monoculture constrains you. You struggle to make decisions that go against its tenets. Conformity seems like an easier, more realistic choice.

But though the monoculture is incredibly pervasive and powerful, it's not the whole story, no matter how much it tries to be. What it means to be human will always encompass more than economic values and assumptions. If you fail to transcend the economic story, you risk paying a heavy internal price. If you do transcend it, you risk paying a heavy external price — but you also gain a chance to live a different kind of life, a chance to help create and sustain the independent life of society that comes from living in a wider spectrum of values.

Your decision matters, because without those other values that have informed humanity for hundreds, even thousands of years, what will happen to us? What will happen to the public interest and the common good? To library faith and intellectual freedom? What will happen to nurturing human dignity, regardless of someone's economic situation? What will happen to how we work for and with each other? To science as the pursuit of the good and the true? To schools and students as teachers and upholders of the civilized society? What will happen to our physical and spiritual health? What will happen to art and to our creativity?

The extent to which these alternate stories and ways of life sound idealistic is the degree to which you've already been influenced by the monoculture. In these other realms of life, as little as thirty years ago, these alternative stories — now derided as idealistic — were objective realities. Today's "idealism" used to be the norm. Now, through the monoculture, we're trading our old aspirations for economic ones.

It's not that the economic story has no place in the world and in our lives — it does. But without these other stories that express other values we have found essential throughout history, we imprison ourselves. When the languages of our other stories begin to be lost, we lose the value diversity and creativity that keeps our society viable. We're left trying to translate something vitally important to us into economic terms so we can justify even talking about it. We end up living a caricature of life, skimming the surface without tasting the fullness. We end up missing what it means to be truly human.

Disconnected from the wholeness of life, we become disconnected from ourselves, from each other, and from the natural world. We struggle to find the meaning in life that we once expressed in non-economic ways. We're left wondering, is this all there is? Because according to the monoculture, only one set of values exists, and those values set the boundaries of the world as we know it.

The monoculture may be overwhelming in its intensity and boundless in its appetite, but its constraints are not inescapable or inevitable. No matter what it tells us over and over about who we are and how we ought to live, we are made of more than one story. Telling a wider truth about where we have come from, who we are, and where we are going lets us live beyond the monoculture's boundaries. Imagine, for a moment, what your life would be if you widened the stream of stories flowing through you, lived beyond economic values and assumptions. How would you experience yourself and others? What kind of work would you choose to do? What would you choose to learn? How would you convey your spirituality? How would you relate to the natural world? What would you create out of the depths of your being?

The story of what has been and what is yet to be lies within each one of us. Wherever you are right now, whatever situation you find yourself in, you have a chance to reflect on your own experience with the monoculture. You have an opportunity to consider how the monoculture is silently shaping the trajectory of your life as you go about your work day after day, interact with others and the natural world, participate in your community, nurture your physical and spiritual health, and continue to learn and create. You have an opportunity to decide, from moment to moment, whether, in your own life, the monoculture's influence will grow or fade. Weigh your options carefully. The decisions you make about how to live and move in the world are the catalysts that will either intensify the monoculture or silently spur other ways of life into being.

The choice is yours.

What stories will you live?

What stories will you tell?

NOTES

1. What Is a Monoculture?

1. Isaiah Berlin, *The Roots of Romanticism: The A.W. Mellon Lectures in the Fine Arts*. Edited by Henry Hardy (Princeton, NJ: Princeton University Press, 1999).

   Additional Sources
   The epigraph is from Robert Fulford's *The Triumph of Narrative* (New York: Broadway Books, 2000).

2. The One Story

1. June Singer's comments on personal mythologies are found in the foreword of David Feinstein and Stanley Krippner's *The Mythic Path* (New York: Putnam Books, 1997).
2. See, for example, Tibor Scitovsky, *The Joyless Economy* (New York: Oxford University Press, 1992).
3. Alan Wolfe, *Whose Keeper? Social Science and Moral Obligation* (Berkeley: University of California Press, 1989).
4. Tibor Scitovsky, *The Joyless Economy* (New York: Oxford University Press, 1992).
5. On being irrational and making wrong decisions systematically, see, for example, Dan Ariely, *Predictably Irrational* (New York: HarperCollins, 2008).

6. See Stephen Marglin, *The Dismal Science: How Thinking Like An Economist Undermines Community* (Cambridge: Harvard University Press, 2008) for more on behavior as an expression of your preferences.

7. Russell Keat, *Cultural Goods and the Limits of the Market* (London: MacMillan Press, 2000).

8. Entrepreneurs are described, for example, in J. Gregory Dees, Jed Emerson and Peter Economy's *Enterprising Nonprofits: A Toolkit for Social Entrepreneurs* (New York: Wiley, 2001).

9. For more on the desire for satisfaction, see Tibor Scitovsky, *The Joyless Economy* (New York: Oxford University Press, 1992).

10. In a world made of markets, even activity that happens outside of markets is described in terms of markets. Nonmarket economics, for example, which examines work that is hard to price because it isn't paid for directly, like cooking and cleaning that happens in the home, defines itself using the market as a reference point: it's not-the-market.

11. As John Kenneth Galbraith said, "To the charge of misuse of power there is the simple, all-embracing answer: your quarrel is with the market. The paradox of power in the classical tradition is, once again, that while all agree that power exists in fact, it does not exist in principle." From his book, *Economics in Perspective: A Critical History* (Boston: Houghton Mifflin, 1987).

12. Market boundaries are described by Russell Keat in *Cultural Goods and the Limits of the Market* (London: MacMillan Press, 2000).

13. For more on choice, see Alan Wolfe's *Whose Keeper? Social Science and Moral Obligation* (Berkeley: University of California Press, 1989).

Additional Sources
The epigraph is from Georg Hegel's *Phenomenology of Spirit* (Oxford: Clarendon Press, 1977).

3. Your Work

1. Peter Cappelli describes the workplace of "the old days" in *The New Deal at Work: Managing the Market-Driven Workforce* (Massachusetts: Harvard Business School Press, 1999). So does

Arne L. Kalleberg in "Nonstandard Employment Relations: Part-time, Temporary and Contract Work," *Annual Review of Sociology* 26 (2000): 341-365.

2. Charles Perrow highlights how many of us are working for organizations in *Organizing America: Wealth, Power, and the Origins of Corporate Capitalism* (Princeton, NJ: Princeton University Press, 2002).

3. Peter Cappelli, *The New Deal at Work: Managing the Market-Driven Workforce* (Massachusetts: Harvard Business School Press, 1999).

4. The pressure organizations are under to compete is described by Brian Becker and Barry Gerhart in "The Impact of Human Resource Management on Organizational Performance: Progress and Prospects," *Academy of Management Journal* 39 (1996): 779-801.

5. Daniel H. Pink describes the rosy world of the free agent in "Free Agent Nation," Fast Company 12 (December 1997).

6. Contingent work is being discussed by a number of researchers, including Anne E. Polivka and Thomas Nardone, "On the definition of 'contingent work,'" *Monthly Labor Review* 112 (1989): 9-16; Arne L. Kalleberg, "Nonstandard Employment Relations: Part-time, Temporary and Contract Work," *Annual Review of Sociology* 26 (2000): 341-365; Catherine E. Connelly and Daniel G. Gallagher, "Emerging Trends in Contingent Work Research," *Journal of Management* 30 (2004): 959-983; Flora Stormer, "The Logic of Contingent Work and Overwork," *Relations Industrielles/Industrial Relations* 63 (2008): 343-362; Arne L. Kalleberg, "Nonstandard Employment Relations: Part-time, Temporary and Contract Work," *Annual Review of Sociology* 26 (2000): 341-365.

7. Anthony Winson and Belinda Leach describe the social effect of contingent work on people's lives in *Contingent Work, Disrupted Lives* (Toronto: University of Toronto Press, 2002), emphasis in original.

8. Peter F. Drucker says business exists to make money compared to other kinds of organizations in *The Practice of Management* (New York: HarperBusiness, 1954).

9. Richard De George, *Business Ethics: Fourth Edition* (New Jersey: Prentice Hall, 1995).

10. For example, in 2007, the conference theme for the Academy of Management (the main professional association for almost 18,000 scholars of management and organizations around the world) was "Doing Well by Doing Good."

11. Flora Stormer, "Making the Shift: Moving From 'Ethics Pays' to an Inter-Systems Model of Business," *Journal of Business Ethics* 44 (2003): 279-289.

12. David Drobis, "Public Relations: Priorities in the Real Economy," *Vital Speeches of the Day* 67 (October 15, 2000: 15-18).

13. Gareth M. Green and Frank Baker, *Work, Health and Productivity* (Oxford: Oxford University Press, 1991).

14. Paul Osterman, 'Work/Family Programs and the Employment Relationship," *Administrative Science Quarterly* 40 (1995): 681-700.

15. Garry A. Gelade and Mark Ivery, "The Impact of Human Resource Management and Work Climate on Organizational Performance," Personnel Psychology 56 (2003): 383-405; Dee W. Edington, "Emerging Research: A View From One Research Center," *American Journal of Health Promotion* 15 (2001): 341-349.

16. For a fascinating overview of how whistleblowing turns out for whistleblowers, see C. Fred Alford's, "Whistle-blowers," *American Behavioral Scientist* 43 (1999): 264-277.

17. The quote, "We hope, through this report and by our future actions, to show that the basic interests of business and society are entirely compatible — that there does not have to be a choice between profits and principles" is found in *The Shell Report 1998*, p. 5, cited in Peter Kok, Ton van der Wiele, Richard McKenna, and Alan A. Brown's "A Corporate Social Responsibility Audit within a Quality Management Framework," *Journal of Business Ethics* 31 (2001: 285-297).

18. Peter Pruzan describes his experience of working with executives and their personal and corporate values in "The Question of Organizational Consciousness: Can Organizations Have Values, Virtues and Visions?" *Journal of Business Ethics* 29 (2001: 271-284).

19. Worker satisfaction, overwork, and burnout are discussed, for example, in Madeleine Bunting's *Willing Slaves: How the Overwork Culture is Ruling Our Lives* (Toronto: HarperCollins,

2004); Richard Brisbois' *How Canada Stacks Up: The Quality of Work — An International Perspective*, Canadian Policy Research Networks, December 19, 2003; and in the Bureau of Labor Statistics, *Issues in Labor Statistics: Twenty-First Century Moonlighters*, U.S. Department of Labor, September 2002.

20. "'Overwork' kills Toyota employee," *BBC News*, July 10, 2008.

21. Johann Hari, "Johann Hari: And now for some good news," *The Independent*, August 6, 2010.

22. Kelley Holland, "Working Long Hours, and Paying a Price," *The New York Times*, July 27, 2008.

23. Deborah L. Rhode, *In the Interests of Justice: Reforming the Legal Profession* (New York: Oxford University Press, 2000); John R. Sapp, *Making Partner: A Guide for Law Firm Associates, Third Edition* (U.S.: American Bar Association Law Practice Management Section, 2006).

24. Deborah L. Rhode, *In the Interests of Justice: Reforming the Legal Profession* (New York: Oxford University Press, 2000).

25. John R. Sapp, *Making Partner: A Guide for Law Firm Associates, Third Edition* (U.S.: American Bar Association Law Practice Management Section, 2006).

26. Robert Devlin describes his 18-hour days in John Bowe, Marisa Bowe, and Sabin Streeter's *Gig: Americans Talk About Their Jobs at the Turn of the Millennium* (New York: Crown, 2000).

27. For an excellent overview of work/life conflict, see Linda Duxbury and Chris Higgins' *Work-Life Balance in the New Millennium*, Canadian Policy Research Networks, October 23, 2001; and Lotte Bailyn, Robert Drago, and Thomas A. Kochan's *Integrating Work and Family Life: A Holistic Approach*, Sloan Work-Family Policy Network, September 14, 2001.

Additional Sources

The first epigraph from the IBM executive is from Peter F. Drucker's *The Practice of Management* (New York: HarperBusiness, 1954).

The second epigraph is from Andrew Grove's *High Output Management* (New York: Vintage, 1995).

4. Your Relationships With Others and the Natural World

1. Alan Wolfe talks about what it means to belong to a group in

Whose Keeper? Social Science and Moral Obligation (Berkeley: University of California Press, 1989).

2. For example, Trudie Knijn, "Marketization and the Struggling Logics of (Home) Care in the Netherlands." In *Care Work: Gender, Class, and the Welfare State*. Edited by Madonna Harrington Meyer (New York: Routledge, 2000), pp. 232-248.

3. Ana Maria Peredo notes that kin relationships were an obstacle to corporate development in "Nothing thicker than blood? Commentary on 'Help one another, use one another: Toward an anthropology of family business,' *Entrepreneurship Theory & Practice* 27 (2003): 397-400; Alan Wolfe, *Whose Keeper? Social Science and Moral Obligation* (Berkeley: University of California Press, 1989).

4. Claudia Goldin describes how women surged into the workforce in *Understanding the Gender Gap: An Economic History of American Women* (New York: Oxford University Press, 1990); so does the U.S. Bureau of the Census, *Statistical Abstract of the U.S.*, Washington, D.C., 2002.

5. Community goals and the dignity of all human beings are traditional focal points in the field of social work. F.G. Reamer, *Ethical Standards in Social Work: A Critical Review of the NASW Code of Ethics* (Washington: NASW Press, 1983), cited in Bob Lonne, Catherine McDonald, Tricia Fox, "Ethical Practice in the Contemporary Human Services," *Journal of Social Work* 4 (2004): 345-367.

6. Alan Wolfe outlines the moral stature of markets and families in *Whose Keeper? Social Science and Moral Obligation* (Berkeley: University of California Press, 1989).

7. Angelika Krebs does a comprehensive job of outlining our justifications for valuing nature in *Ethics of Nature* (Berlin: Walter de Gruyter, 1999).

8. Zygmunt Bauman's description of reality television appears in *Society Under Siege* (Cambridge, UK: Polity Press, 2002).

9. Sheila Riddell and Alastair Wilson explore how people with learning difficulties are "deemed to be of only marginal economic value" in "Captured Customers: People with Learning Difficulties in the Social Market," *British Educational Research Journal* 25 (1999): 445-461.

10. Claudia Goldin, *Understanding the Gender Gap: An Economic History of American Women* (New York: Oxford University Press, 1990); U.S. Bureau of the Census, *Statistical Abstract of the U.S.*, Washington, D.C., 2002.

11. Arlie Russell Hochschild, *The Time Bind: When Work Becomes Home and Home Becomes Work* (New York: Metropolitan Books, 1997).

12. Suzanne M. Bianchi, John P. Robinson, Melissa A. Milkie, *Changing Rhythms in American Family Life* (New York: Russell Sage Foundation, 2007); Alan Wolfe, *Whose Keeper? Social Science and Moral Obligation* (Berkeley: University of California Press, 1989).

13. Pamela Paul discusses the reasons people give for having fewer children in "Childless by Choice," *American Demographics* 23 (2001): 44-50; Arlie Russell Hochschild describes "time famine" in *The Time Bind: When Work Becomes Home and Home Becomes Work* (New York: Metropolitan Books, 1997).

14. Sylvia Ann Hewlett's discussion of how professional life impacts family is found in "Executive Women and the Myth of Having It All," *Harvard Business Review* 80 (2002).

15. Non-market economist Nancy Folbre points out the link between having a family and economic vulnerability in *The Invisible Heart: Economics and Family Values* (New York: New Press, 2001).

16. Charles Taylor, *The Malaise of Modernity* (Toronto: Anansi Press, 1991).

17. Stephen Marglin, *The Dismal Science: How Thinking Like An Economist Undermines Community* (Cambridge: Harvard University Press, 2008).

18. Trudie Knijn, "Marketization and the Struggling Logics of (Home) Care in the Netherlands." In *Care Work: Gender, Class, and the Welfare State*. Edited by Madonna Harrington Meyer (New York: Routledge, 2000), pp. 232-248.

19. Mary Pipher, "In Praise of Hometowns." In *Sustainable Planet: Solutions for the Twenty-First Century*. Edited by Juliet B. Schor and Betsy Taylor (Boston: Beacon Press, 2002).

20. The link between mobility and economic development is discussed in the World Business Council for Sustainable

Development's *Mobility for Development: Facts and Trends*, September 2007. For example, North Americans travelled 40 miles a day on average (mostly by car and plane) in 2007, compared to seven miles for Brazilians (by car and bus), and 3 miles for Tanzanians (by foot, bus, and bicycle).

21. F. M. Deutsch, *Halving It All: How Equally Shared Parenting Works* (Cambridge, MA: Harvard University Press), quoted in Lotte Bailyn, Robert Drago, and Thomas A. Kochan, *Integrating Work and Family Life: A Holistic Approach, A Report of the Sloan Work-Family Policy Network* (2002); Nancy Folbre, *The Invisible Heart: Economics and Family Values* (New York: New Press, 2001).

22. Tom Peters introduces "The Brand Called You" in *Fast Company* 10 (1997).

23. Fritz Pappenheim discusses Ferdinand Tonies' *Gesellschaft* versus *Gemeinschaft* in "Alienation in American Society," *Monthly Review* June (2000).

24. Social entrepreneurship is described by Johanna Mair and Ignasi Marti, "Social Entrepreneurship Research: A Source of Explanation, Prediction, and Delight," *Journal of World Business* 41(2006): 36-44; and by Thomas Reis and Stephanie Clohesy, *Unleashing New Resources and Entrepreneurship for the Common Good* (Battle Creek, Michigan: Kellogg Foundation, 1999).

25. Gregory Dees warns nonprofits about the risks of becoming business-oriented in "Enterprising Nonprofits," *Harvard Business Review*, January (1998): 54-67; John Catford, "Social Entrepreneurs are Vital for Health Promotion — but They Need Supportive Environments Too," *Health Promotion International* 13 (1998): 95-97.

26. The quote about thousands of organizations in the U.S. experimenting with market-based approaches to social problems appears in Thomas Reis and Stephanie Clohesy's *Unleashing New Resources and Entrepreneurship for the Common Good* (Battle Creek, Michigan: Kellogg Foundation, 1999).

27. Kurt Aschermann, "The Ten Commandments of Cause-Related Marketing," *Cause Marketing Forum*, www.causemarketingforum.com, undated.

28. Ben Gose, "A Revolution was Ventured, But What Did It Gain?" *Chronicle of Philanthropy* 15 (2003): 6-9.

29. Ibid.
30. Angela M. Eikenberry, and Jodie Drapal Kluver explain what the nonprofit sector used to be about in "The Marketization of the Nonprofit Sector: Civil Society at Risk?" *Public Administration Review* 64 (2004): 132-140.
31. An argument for economic growth preceding social and spiritual wealth is found in Thomas Reis and Stephanie Clohesy's *Unleashing New Resources and Entrepreneurship for the Common Good* (Battle Creek, Michigan: Kellogg Foundation, 1999).
32. For more on the environment and the economy, see Mark Sagoff, *The Economy of the Earth* (New York: Cambridge University Press, 2008); Gretchen C. Daily, *Nature's Services: Societal Dependence on Natural Ecosystems* (Washington, DC: Island Press, 1997); Harold A. Mooney and Paul R. Ehrlich, "Ecosystem Services: A Fragmentary History," in *Nature's Services: Societal Dependence on Natural Ecosystems.* Edited by Gretchen C. Daily (Washington, DC: Island Press; 1997), pp. 11-19.
33. The detailed descriptions of what goods and services are provided to us by the earth's ecosystems is from the National Geographic website, *Our Relationship With Nature, A Fragile System Sustains Us: Nature Reveals Its True Value,* http://www.nationalgeographic.com/earthpulse/ecosystem-and-conservation.html, undated.
34. The Economics of Ecosystems and Biodiversity (TEEB) report that came out of the meeting of the G8+5 Environment Ministers in Germany in 2007 is discussed by National Geographic in "Ecosystem Investments Could Yield Trillions of Dollars in Benefits, Study Finds," *NATGEO Newswatch*, November 13, 2009. The TEEB report is available at www.teebweb.org.
35. *Stanford Report*, "Q&A with Gretchen Daily, Woods Institute Fellow and Professor of Biological Sciences," August 2, 2007.
36. Ibid.
37. Thomas L. Friedman, *The Lexus and the Olive Tree: Understanding Globalization* (New York: Farrar Straus Giroux, 1999).

Additional Sources

The first epigraph is from Robert Solomon's *Love: Emotion,*

Myth and Metaphor (New York: Doubleday, 1981).

The second epigraph is from Jonathan Amos' "Study Limits Maximum Tree Height," *BBC News*, April 21, 2004.

5. Your Community

1. See, for example, Lawrence Pratchett and Melvin Wingfield. "Petty Bureaucracy and Woolly-minded Liberalism? The Changing Ethos of Local Government Officers," *Public Adminstration* 74 (1996): 639-656.

2. See Laurence E. Lynn Jr., *Public Management: Old and New* (New York: Routledge, 2006), for an excellent overview of the rise of New Public Management.

3. Sandford Borins, "New Public Management, North American Style." In *New Public Management: Current Trends and Future Prospects*. Edited by Kate McLaughlin, Stephen P. Osborne, and Ewan Ferlie (London: Routledge, 2002), pp. 181-194.

4. Sandra Dawson and Charlotte Dargie, "New Public Management: A Discussion with Special Reference to UK Health." In *New Public Management: Current Trends and Future Prospects*. Edited by Kate McLaughlin, Stephen P. Osborne, and Ewan Ferlie (London: Routledge, 2002), pp. 34-56.

5. Laurence E. Lynn Jr., *Public Management: Old and New* (New York: Routledge, 2006); Stephen P. Osborne and Kate McLaughlin, "The New Public Management in Context." In *New Public Management: Current Trends and Future Prospects*. Edited by Kate McLaughlin, Stephen P. Osborne, and Ewan Ferlie (London: Routledge, 2002), pp. 7-14.

6. Laurence E. Lynn Jr., *Public Management: Old and New* (New York: Routledge, 2006); Sandra Dawson and Charlotte Dargie, "New Public Management: A Discussion with Special Reference to UK Health." In *New Public Management: Current Trends and Future Prospects*. Edited by Kate McLaughlin, Stephen P. Osborne, and Ewan Ferlie (London: Routledge, 2002), pp. 34-56.

7. Laurence E. Lynn Jr., *Public Management: Old and New* (New York: Routledge, 2006).

8. Jane Broadbent and Richard Laughlin, "Public Service Professionals and the New Public Management: Control of the Professions in the Public Services." In *New Public Management:*

Current Trends and Future Prospects. Edited by Kate McLaughlin, Stephen P. Osborne, and Ewan Ferlie (London: Routledge, 2002), pp. 95-108.

9. Stephen P. Osborne and Kate McLaughlin describe how the jury is still out on whether or not New Public Management improves government efficiency in "The New Public Management in Context." In *New Public Management: Current Trends and Future Prospects*. Edited by Kate McLaughlin, Stephen P. Osborne, and Ewan Ferlie (London: Routledge, 2002), pp. 7-14.

10. David D. Friedman describes efficiency as the answer to the question "What should we do?" in *Law's Order: What Economics Has to do With Law and Why It Matters* (Princeton, NJ: Princeton University Press, 2000).

11. David Shichor, *Punishment for Profit* (Thousand Oaks, CA: Sage, 1995). In the Middle Ages in England, if you were a victim of a crime and wanted to do something about it, you hired a private prosecutor and paid for the prosecution yourself.

12. Ibid.

13. The reasons behind incarceration are outlined by Norval Morris and David J. Rothman in their introduction to *The Oxford History of the Prison: The Practice of Punishment in Western Society*. Edited by Norval Morris and David J. Rothman (New York: Oxford University Press, 1995).

14. David Shichor, *Punishment for Profit* (Thousand Oaks, CA: Sage, 1995).

15. For more on privatized prisons, see James Austin and Garry Coventry's report *Emerging Issues on Privatized Prisons* (San Francisco, CA: National Council on Crime and Delinquency, 2001).

16. David J. Rothman describes prison labor in "Perfecting the Prison: United States, 1789-1865." In *The Oxford History of the Prison: The Practice of Punishment in Western Society*. Edited by Norval Morris and David J. Rothman (New York: Oxford University Press, 1995); David Shichor, *Punishment for Profit* (Thousand Oaks, CA: Sage, 1995).

17. U.S. prisoners per capita in 1992: 455, compared to South Africa's 332, Canada's 109, and Sweden's 61. Norval Morris, "The Contemporary Prison: 1965-Present." In *The Oxford History of the Prison: The Practice of Punishment in Western Society*. Edited

by Norval Morris and David J. Rothman (New York: Oxford University Press, 1995).

18. The justifications for prison privatization are described by David Shichor in *Punishment for Profit* (Thousand Oaks, CA: Sage, 1995).

19. Ibid.

20. James Austin and Garry Coventry, *Emerging Issues on Privatized Prisons* (San Francisco, CA: National Council on Crime and Delinquency, 2001); David Shichor, *Punishment for Profit* (Thousand Oaks, CA: Sage, 1995).

21. For more on the debatable success of privatized prisons and lower wages and benefits paid to staff, see James Austin and Garry Coventry's *Emerging Issues on Privatized Prisons* (San Francisco, CA: National Council on Crime and Delinquency, 2001). Overtime is particularly burdensome because of high staff turnover. California prison guards, for example, averaged $57,000 a year in base pay in 2005; with overtime pay, 2,400 guards made over $100,000, and the highest paid correctional guard made $187,000. (Steve Schmidt, "Prison Guards Lock Up Bundle in OT Pay," *San Diego Union Tribune*, February 28, 2006.)

22. Gary Paulsen, in an author profile compiled by ipl2, http://www.ipl.org/div/askauthor/paulsen.html.

23. Isaac Asimov, *I. Asimov, a Memoir* (New York: Doubleday, 1994).

24. Oliver Garceau, *The Public Library in the Political Process* (New York: Columbia University Press, 1949).

25. Ronald McCabe, *Civic Librarianship: Renewing the Social Mission of the Public Library* (Lanham, MD: Scarecrow Press, 2001).

26. For more on libraries and their role in a democratic society, see Molly Raphael, "Why Do Libraries Matter in the 21st Century?" In *Perspectives, Insights & Priorities: 17 Leaders Speak Freely of Librarianship*. Edited by Norman Horrocks (Lanham, MD: Scarecrow Press, 2005), pp. 115-122; Ed D'Angelo, *Barbarians at the Gates of the Public Library* (Duluth, MN: Library Juice Press, 2006).

27. The statement by the Boston Public Library trustees is cited

by John N. Berry III, "Election 2004: The Library Fails Again." In *Perspectives, Insights & Priorities: 17 Leaders Speak Freely of Librarianship*. Edited by Norman Horrocks (Lanham, MD: Scarecrow Press, 2005), pp. 13-18.

28. United Nations Educational, Scientific, and Cultural Organization, "UNESCO Public Library Manifesto."

29. For more on the library, the public good, and society, see Michael Gorman, "Library Values in a Changing World." In *Perspectives, Insights & Priorities: 17 Leaders Speak Freely of Librarianship*. Edited by Norman Horrocks (Lanham, MD: Scarecrow Press, 2005), pp. 55-62; Evelyn M. Campbell, Suzanne Duncan, Sonal Rastogi, and Joan Wilson, "The Future is Now: Will Public Libraries Survive?" In *Reinvention of the Public Library for the 21st Century*. Edited by William L. Whitesides Sr., (Englewood, CO: Libraries Unlimited, 1998), pp. 180-204.

30. Samuel E. Trosow and Kirsti Nilsen, *Constraining Public Libraries: The World Trade Organization's General Agreement on Trade in Services* (Lanham, MD: Scarecrow Press, 2006).

31. Herbert I. Schiller, Culture, Inc. (Oxford: Oxford University Press, 1989); Michael Gorman, "Library Values in a Changing World." In *Perspectives, Insights & Priorities: 17 Leaders Speak Freely of Librarianship*. Edited by Norman Horrocks (Lanham, MD: Scarecrow Press, 2005), pp. 55-62.

32. American Library Association Office of Intellectual Freedom, "The Freedom to Read Statement."

33. The ALA keeps an annual list of the most challenged books in library collections. Leigh S. Estabrook, "A Virtuous Profession." In *Perspectives, Insights & Priorities: 17 Leaders Speak Freely of Librarianship*. Edited by Norman Horrocks (Lanham, MD: Scarecrow Press, 2005), pp. 43-48; Ann K. Symons, "The More Things Change, the More Things Remain the Same." In *Perspectives, Insights & Priorities: 17 Leaders Speak Freely of Librarianship*. Edited by Norman Horrocks (Lanham, MD: Scarecrow Press, 2005), pp. 123-130. This is why many librarians were against the United States' 2001 Patriot Act.

34. Herbert I. Schiller describes how libraries create information resources that markets don't in *Culture, Inc.* (Oxford: Oxford University Press, 1989).

35. Camila Alire, "The Library Professional." In *Perspectives, Insights & Priorities: 17 Leaders Speak Freely of Librarianship*. Edited by Norman Horrocks (Lanham, MD: Scarecrow Press, 2005), pp. 55-62.

36. Ronald McCabe, *Civic Librarianship: Renewing the Social Mission of the Public Library* (Lanham, MD: Scarecrow Press, 2001).

37. In the first decade of the twenty-first century, the top banned or challenged books included J.K. Rowling's *Harry Potter* series, John Steinbeck's *Of Mice and Men*, Maya Angelou's *I Know Why the Caged Bird Sings*, Mark Twain's *The Adventures of Huckleberry Finn*, J.D. Salinger's *Catcher in the Rye*, and Aldous Huxley's *Brave New World*. For each documented challenge, as many as four or five go unreported. American Library Association, "Top 100 Banned/Challenged Books: 2000-2009."

38. Ken Haycock, "Librarianship: Intersecting Perspectives for the Academy and From the Field." In *Perspectives, Insights & Priorities: 17 Leaders Speak Freely of Librarianship*. Edited by Norman Horrocks (Lanham, MD: Scarecrow Press, 2005), pp. 63-72.

39. Steve Coffman asked, "What If You Ran Your Library Like a Bookstore?" in *American Libraries* 29 (1998): 40-46; Megan Lane highlights libraries as Idea Stores in "Is This the Library of the Future?" *BBC News*, March 18, 2003.

40. Ruth Rikowski, "The Corporate Takeover of Libraries," *Information for Social Change* 14; Ronald McCabe, *Civic Librarianship: Renewing the Social Mission of the Public Library* (Lanham, MD: Scarecrow Press, 2001).

41. Overdue fines for late books weren't counted as fees because library users could avoid the fines by returning the books on time. Samuel E. Trosow and Kirsti Nilsen, *Constraining Public Libraries: The World Trade Organization's General Agreement on Trade in Services* (Lanham, MD: Scarecrow Press, 2006).

42. Jason Hammond highlights user fees in public libraries in "Cash Cow: User Fees in Alberta Public Libraries," *Partnership: the Canadian Journal of Library and Information Practice and Research* 2 (2007).

43. Shelley Mardiros documents the town of Banff's experience with library user fees in "Banff's Very Public Library," *Alberta Views* 4 (2001): 37-39.

44. Jason Hammond, "Cash Cow: User Fees in Alberta Public Libraries," *Partnership: the Canadian Journal of Library and Information Practice and Research* 2 (2007).

45. Samuel E. Trosow and Kirsti Nilsen, *Constraining Public Libraries: The World Trade Organization's General Agreement on Trade in Services* (Lanham, MD: Scarecrow Press, 2006).

46. Geoff Dembicki, "Librarians Told to Stand on Guard for 2010 Sponsors," *The Tyee*, January 12, 2010.

47. For more on outsourcing in public libraries, see Samuel E. Trosow and Kirsti Nilsen's *Constraining Public Libraries: The World Trade Organization's General Agreement on Trade in Services* (Lanham, MD: Scarecrow Press, 2006).

48. Samuel E. Trosow and Kirsti Nilsen, *Constraining Public Libraries: The World Trade Organization's General Agreement on Trade in Services* (Lanham, MD: Scarecrow Press, 2006); Norman Oder, "When LSSI Comes to Town," *Library Journal*, October 1, 2004.

49. David Streitfeld, "Anger as a Private Company takes Over Libraries," *The New York Times*, September 26, 2010.

Additional Sources
The first epigraph is from *The Political Writings of John Adams*. Edited by George W. Carey (Washington, DC: Regnery Publishing, 2000).
The second epigraph, a quote by Mike Smith, was reported by Kelly Regan in "Fossil Fuels Official Gives Oil, Gas Support," *Charleston Gazette*, January 31, 2002.

6. Your Physical and Spiritual Health

1. Daniel Callahan defines health and cites Plato's view of doctors in his book *False Hopes: Why America's Quest For Perfect Health is a Recipe for Failure* (New York: Simon & Schuster, 1998).

2. Paul Starr, *The Social Transformation of American Medicine* (New York: Basic Books, 1982).

3. Anne Stoline and Jonathan P. Weiner, *The New Medical Marketplace: A Physician's Guide to the Health Care Revolution* (Baltimore: Johns Hopkins University Press, 1988).

4. Ibid.

5. Paul Starr, *The Social Transformation of American Medicine*

(New York: Basic Books, 1982).

6. Anne Stoline and Jonathan P. Weiner, *The New Medical Marketplace: A Physician's Guide to the Health Care Revolution* (Baltimore: Johns Hopkins University Press, 1988).

7. Paul Starr, *The Social Transformation of American Medicine* (New York: Basic Books, 1982).

8. The ethics code of the American Medical Association is highlighted by Paul Starr in *The Social Transformation of American Medicine* (New York: Basic Books, 1982).

9. Anne Stoline and Jonathan P. Weiner, *The New Medical Marketplace: A Physician's Guide to the Health Care Revolution* (Baltimore: Johns Hopkins University Press, 1988); seeing different specialists "fragments the patient."

10. Daniel Callahan, *False Hopes: Why America's Quest For Perfect Health is a Recipe for Failure* (New York: Simon & Schuster, 1998).

11. Eliot Freidson, *Medical Work in America: Essays on Health Care* (New Haven: Yale University Press, 1989).

12. Anne Stoline and Jonathan P. Weiner, *The New Medical Marketplace: A Physician's Guide to the Health Care Revolution* (Baltimore: Johns Hopkins University Press, 1988).

13. Interestingly, technology had the same effect of increasing costs instead of decreasing them in museums too, through expensive developments in museum lighting, and temperature and humidity control.

14. B. H. Gray and W. J. McNerney compare old doctors' hospitals to family farms in "For-profit Enterprise in Health Care. The Institute of Medicine Study," *New England Journal of Medicine* 314 (1986): 1523-28.

15. Rosemary Stevens highlights the growth in stock price in multinational health care companies in *In Sickness and in Wealth: American Hospitals in the Twentieth Century* (Baltimore: Johns Hopkins University Press, 1999).

16. Anne Stoline and Jonathan P. Weiner, *The New Medical Marketplace: A Physician's Guide to the Health Care Revolution* (Baltimore: Johns Hopkins University Press, 1988).

17. Arnold S. Relman, *A Second Opinion* (New York: Public Affairs, 2007); Rosemary Stevens, *In Sickness and in Wealth: American Hospitals in the Twentieth Century* (Baltimore: Johns Hopkins

University Press, 1999).

18. For examples of health care policy laid out by business school professors and economists, see Regina Herzlinger (Harvard Business School economist), *Who Killed Health Care? America's $2 Trillion Dollar Medical Problem — And the Consumer-Driven Cure* (New York: McGraw-Hill, 2007); Michael E. Porter and Elizabeth Olmsted Teisberg (business school professors of strategy, competitiveness and innovation), *Redefining Health Care: Creating Value-Based Competition on Results* (Cambridge: Harvard Business School Press, 2006).

19. Arnold S. Relman, *A Second Opinion* (New York: Public Affairs, 2007).

20. Daniel Callahan, *False Hopes: Why America's Quest For Perfect Health is a Recipe for Failure* (New York: Simon & Schuster, 1998).

21. Paul Starr, *The Social Transformation of American Medicine* (New York: Basic Books, 1982).

22. American Medical Association 1966 Opinions and Reports of the Judicial Council, cited in Arnold S. Relman, *A Second Opinion* (New York: Public Affairs, 2007).

23. Eliot Freidson, *Medical Work in America: Essays on Health Care* (New Haven: Yale University Press, 1989).

24. Rosemary Stevens, *American Medicine and the Public Interest* (New Haven: Yale University Press, 1971); Anne Stoline and Jonathan P. Weiner, *The New Medical Marketplace: A Physician's Guide to the Health Care Revolution* (Baltimore: Johns Hopkins University Press, 1988); Eliot Freidson, *Medical Work in America: Essays on Health Care* (New Haven: Yale University Press, 1989).

25. Daniel Callahan, *False Hopes: Why America's Quest For Perfect Health is a Recipe for Failure* (New York: Simon & Schuster, 1998).

26. Rosemary Stevens, *In Sickness and in Wealth: American Hospitals in the Twentieth Century* (Baltimore: Johns Hopkins University Press, 1999).

27. Paul Basken, "Medical Journals See a Cost to Fighting Industry-Backed Research," *Chronicle of Higher Education*, September 13, 2009.

28. Duff Wilson and Natasha Singer, "Ghostwriting is Called Rife

in Medical Journals," *The New York Times*, September 11, 2009.

29. Ibid.

30. The national survey of doctors' relationships with industry is described in Ibby Caputo's "Probing Doctors' Ties to Industry," *The Washington Post*, August 18, 2009.

31. For more on medical bankruptcies in the U.S., see David U. Himmelstein, Deborah Thorne, Elizabeth Warren, and Steffie Woolhandler's "Medical Bankruptcy in the United States, 2007: Results of a National Study," *American Journal of Medicine* 122 (2009): 741-746.

32. Paul Starr, *The Social Transformation of American Medicine* (New York: Basic Books, 1982).

33. Arnold S. Relman, *A Second Opinion* (New York: Public Affairs, 2007).

34. Daniel Callahan, *False Hopes: Why America's Quest For Perfect Health is a Recipe for Failure* (New York: Simon & Schuster, 1998).

35. James W. Fowler quotes Wilfred Cantwell Smith's version of faith in *Stages of Faith: The Psychology of Human Development and the Quest for Meaning* (New York: HarperCollins, 1995).

36. The Pew Forum on Religion and Public Life, "U.S. Religious Landscape Survey," 2007.

37. Diana Butler Bass does an excellent job of highlighting Christian beliefs through distinct historical periods in *A People's History of Christianity* (New York: HarperOne, 2007).

38. Ibid.

39. Ibid.

40. For more on the Protestant work ethic, see Max Weber's classic, *The Protestant Ethic and the Spirit of Capitalism* (New York: Scribner, 1976); Diana Butler Bass, *A People's History of Christianity* (New York: HarperOne, 2007).

41. Diana Butler Bass, *A People's History of Christianity* (New York: HarperOne, 2007).

42. Ibid.

43. Michael Budde and Robert Brimlow, *Christianity Incorporated* (Grand Rapids, MI: Brazos Press, 2002); John B. Cobb, Jr., *Sustaining the Common Good* (Cleveland: Pilgrim Press, 1994).

44. Religious market theory is laid out in detail in Roger Finke, Avery M. Guest, and Rodney Stark's "Mobilizing local religious markets: Religious pluralism in the empire state, 1855-1865," *American Sociological Review* 61 (1996): 203-218.

45. For example: Rodney Stark, Roger Finke, and Laurence Iannaccone, "Pluralism and piety: England and Wales, 1851," *Journal for the Scientific Study of Religion* 34 (1995): 431-444; Roger Finke, Avery M. Guest, and Rodney Stark, "Mobilizing local religious markets: Religious pluralism in the empire state, 1855-1865," *American Sociological Review* 61 (1996): 203-218.

46. Roger Finke, Avery M. Guest, and Rodney Stark, "Mobilizing local religious markets: Religious pluralism in the empire state, 1855-1865," *American Sociological Review* 61 (1996): 203-218.

47. "Jesus, CEO; Churches as Businesses," *The Economist* 377 (2005): 41-44.

48. Kirbyjon Caldwell and Walt Kallestad, *Entrepreneurial Faith* (Colorado Springs: Waterbrook Press, 2004).

49. The quote from the former executive vice president and business manager of the Billy Graham Evangelistic Association is found in *Billy Graham, God's Ambassador* (New York: HarperOne, 2007).

50. "Product Placement in the Pews? Microtargeting meets Megachurches," Knowledge@Wharton, November 15, 2006.

51. Ibid.

52. "Product Placement in the Pews? Microtargeting meets Megachurches," Knowledge@Wharton, November 15, 2006; Michael L. Budde, "Collecting Praise: Global Culture Industries." In *The Blackwell Companion to Christian Ethics*. Edited by Stanley Hauerwas and Samuel Wells (Malden, MA: Blackwell, 2004), pp. 123-137.

53. Michael L. Budde, "Collecting Praise: Global Culture Industries." In *The Blackwell Companion to Christian Ethics*. Edited by Stanley Hauerwas and Samuel Wells (Malden, MA: Blackwell, 2004), pp. 123-137; Perry Dane, "The Corporation Sole and the Encounter of Law and Church." In *Sacred Companies*. Edited by N. J. Demerath III, Peter Dobkin Hall, Terry Schmitt, and Rhys

H. Williams (Oxford, Oxford University Press: 1998).

54. Darrell Guder, *The Continuing Conversion of the Church* (Grand Rapids, Michigan: William B. Eerdmans, 2000).

55. Philip D. Kenneson and James L. Street, *Selling Out the Church* (Eugene, Oregon: Wipf & Stock, 2003).

Additional Sources

The first epigraph is from E.F. Schumacher's *Small is Beautiful* (New York: Harper & Row, 1973).

The second epigraph is from Mother Teresa's *No Greater Love* (New York: New World Library, 2002).

7. Your Education

1. A great number of scholars are talking about the market's effect in higher education. See, for example, Douglas M. Priest and Edward P. St. John, *Privatization and Public Universities* (Bloomington: Indiana University Press, 2006); Edward P. St. John and Ontario S. Wooden, "Privatization and Federal Funding for Higher Education." In *Privatization and Public Universities*. Edited by Douglas M. Priest and Edward P. St. John (Bloomington: Indiana University Press, 2006), pp. 38-64; Susan Wright, "Markets, Corporations, Consumers? New Landscapes of Higher Education," *Learning & Teaching in the Social Sciences* 1(2004): 71-93; Brian Pusser, "Higher Education, Markets, and the Preservation of the Public Good." In *Earnings From Learning*. Edited by David W. Breneman, Brian Pusser, and Sarah E. Turner (New York: State University of New York Press, 2006), pp. 23-49.

2. For more on the history of scientific knowledge, see Jerome R. Ravetz, *Scientific Knowledge and its Social Problems* (New York: Oxford University Press, 1971).

3. The commercialization of knowledge is described in Joshua B. Powers' "Patents and Royalties," In *Privatization and Public Universities*. Edited by Douglas M. Priest and Edward P. St. John (Bloomington: Indiana University Press, 2006), pp. 129-150.

4. For a succinct outline of Robert Merton's four scientific norms, see Bruce Macfarlane and Ming Cheng, "Communism, Universalism and Disinterestedness: Re-examining Contemporary Support

Among Academics for Merton's Scientific Norms," *Journal of Academic Ethics*, 6 (2008): 67-78.

5. Galileo's statement about truth and science is found in Galileo Galilei, *Dialogue on the Great World Systems, The Salusbury Translation*. Edited by G. de Santillana, (Chicago: University of Chicago Press, 1953), cited in Jerome R. Ravetz, *Scientific Knowledge and its Social Problems* (New York: Oxford University Press, 1971).

6. Jerome R. Ravetz, *Scientific Knowledge and its Social Problems* (New York: Oxford University Press, 1971).

7. Regarding the education services industry, in 2003, America's non-profit higher education sector was made of almost 4,000 organizations representing roughly 1.4 million students and annual expenditures of over $200 billion. David W. Breneman, Brian Pusser, and Sarah E. Turner, "The Contemporary Provision of For-Profit Higher Education." In *Earnings From Learning*. Edited by David W. Breneman, Brian Pusser, and Sarah E. Turner (New York: State University of New York Press, 2006), pp. 3-22.

8. "Arts Degrees 'Reduce Earnings,'" *BBC News*, March 6, 2003.

9. Ibid.

10. Jason Tan, "The Marketisation of Education in Singapore: Policies and Implications," *International Review of Education* 44 (1998): 47-63; Ka-ho Mok, "Education and the Market Place in Hong Kong and Mainland China," *Higher Education* 37 (1999): 133-158; Yin Qiping, "The 'Marketisation' of Chinese Higher Education: A Critical Assessment," *Comparative Education*, 30 (1994): 217-233.

11. Rising tuition rates for professional programs in Canada is highlighted by Marc Frenette in "The Impact of Tuition Fees on University Access: Evidence From a Large-Scale Price Deregulation in Professional Programs," *Statistics Canada* 11F0019MIE - Number 263 (2005).

12. For more on changes in financial aid, see Sean Junor and Alex Usher, "The End of Need-Based Student Financial Aid in Canada?" *Educational Policy Institute* (2007); "Canadian Millennium Scholarship Foundation," Brief Submitted to The House of Commons Standing Committee on Finance 2006 Pre-

Budget Consultations.

13. Douglas M. Priest and Edward P. St. John, *Privatization and Public Universities* (Bloomington: Indiana University Press, 2006).

14. Simon Marginson, "National and Global Competition in Higher Education," *Australian Educational Researcher* 31 (2004): 1-28.

15. Sally Power and Geoff Whitty, "Teaching New Subjects? The Hidden Curriculum of Marketized Education Systems." Paper presented at the annual meeting of the American Educational Research Association, Chicago, Illinois, March 24-28, 1997.

16. Michael Pearce, "The Marketization of Discourse About Education in UK General Election Manifestos," *Text* 24 (2004): 245-265; Ingolfur Asgeir Johannesson, Sverker Lindblad, and Hannu Simola, "An Inevitable Progress? Educational Restructuring in Finland, Iceland, and Sweden at the Turn of the Millennium," *Scandinavian Journal of Educational Research* 46 (2002): 325-339; Izhar Oplatka, Jane Hesley-Brown, and Nick H. Foskett, "The Voice of Teachers in Marketing Their School: Personal Perspectives in Competitive Environments," *School Leadership & Management* 22 (2002): 177-196.

17. Brian Pusser, "Higher Education, Markets, and the Preservation of the Public Good." In *Earnings From Learning*. Edited by David W. Breneman, Brian Pusser, and Sarah E. Turner (New York: State University of New York Press, 2006), pp. 23-49; Kathryn Hibbert and Luigi Iannacci, "From Dissemination to Discernment: The Commodification of Literacy Instruction and the Fostering of Good Teacher Consumerism," *Reading Teacher* 58 (2005): 716-727; Susan Wright, "Markets, Corporations, Consumers? New Landscapes of Higher Education," *Learning & Teaching in the Social Sciences* 1 (2004): 71-93; Ka-ho Mok, "Education and the Market Place in Hong Kong and Mainland China," *Higher Education* 37 (1999): 133-158.

18. For an excellent and early overview of the spread and influence of the market in higher education, see Sheila Slaughter and Gary Rhoades, *Academic Capitalism and the New Economy* (Baltimore: Johns Hopkins University Press, 2004).

19. Douglas M. Priest and Rachel Dykstra Boon, "Incentive-based Budgeting Systems in the Emerging Environment." In *Earnings*

From Learning. Edited by David W. Breneman, Brian Pusser, and Sarah E. Turner (New York: State University of New York Press, 2006), pp. 175-188.

20. The statistical decline in tenure and tenure-track faculty positions is found in the 2006 Contingent Faculty Index, put out by the American Association of University Professors, cited in Peter Conn, "We Need to Acknowledge the Realities of Employment in the Humanities," *The Chronicle Review,* April 4, 2010.

21. Marc Bousquet outlines how job security in academia has been impacted by marketization in his book *How the University Works: Higher Education and the Low-Wage Nation* (New York: New York University Press, 2008).

22. Marc Bousquet, *How the University Works: Higher Education and the Low-Wage Nation* (New York: New York University Press, 2008). See also Sheila Slaughter and Larry L. Leslie, *Academic Capitalism: Politics, Policies, and the Entrepreneurial University* (Baltimore: Johns Hopkins University Press, 1997).

23. The rise of economic language in academia is described by Fazal Rizvi, "The Ideology of Privatization in Higher Education: A Global Perspective." In *Earnings From Learning.* Edited by David W. Breneman, Brian Pusser, and Sarah E. Turner (New York: State University of New York Press, 2006), pp. 65-84; Peter Roberts, "The Future of the University: Reflections from New Zealand," *International Review of Education* 45 (1999): 65-86; Ka-ho Mok, "The Cost of Managerialism: The Implications for the 'McDonaldisation' of Higher Education in Hong Kong," *Journal of Higher Education Policy* 21 (1999): 117-127.

24. Jerome R. Ravetz, *Scientific Knowledge and its Social Problems* (New York: Oxford University Press, 1971).

25. Ibid.

26. On knowledge commercialization and science and industry partnerships, see, for example, Eyal Press and Jennifer Washburn, "The Kept University," *Atlantic Monthly* 285 (2000): 39-53; David Blumenthal, Eric G. Campbell, NancyAnne Causino, and Karen Seashore Louis, "Participation of Life-Science Faculty in Research Relationships with Industry," *New England Journal of Medicine* 335 (1996): 1734-1739.

27. Eric G. Campbell, Joshua B. Powers, David Blumenthal, and

Brian Biles, "Inside the Triple Helix: Technology Transfer and Commercialization in the Life Sciences," *Health Affairs* 23 (2004): 64-76. Today, most commercialization activity happens in the biosciences. In 2001, almost half of academic patents in the U.S. were from the life sciences in chemistry, molecular biology, and microbiology, up from 15 percent in 1980.

28. On the salary gap between business schools and the humanities, see James Engell and Anthony Dangerfield, "The Market-Model University: Humanities in the Age of Money," *Harvard Alumni Magazine* (May/June 1998).

29. See, for example, Robert N. Watson's "The Humanities Really Do Produce a Profit," *Chronicle of Higher Education*, March 21, 2010.

30. John Mursell, *Principles of Democratic Education* (New York: W.W. Norton, 1955).

31. Clifford Geertz, *Available Light* (Princeton, NJ: Princeton University Press, 2000).

Additional Sources
The first epigraph, a quote from then-93-year-old Sophie Mumford, is found in Studs Terkel's *Coming of Age* (New York: New Press, 1995).
John Lombardi is quoted in Marc Bousquet's *How the University Works: Higher Education and the Low-Wage Nation* (New York: New York University Press, 2008).

8. Your Creativity

1. For a wonderful overview of the history of the idea of art, see Larry Shiner's *The Invention of Art: A Cultural History* (Chicago: University of Chicago Press, 2001).

2. Ibid.

3. The Louvre in Paris opened in 1973 with art that had been confiscated from the monarchy and the aristocracy during the French Revolution. See Larry Shiner, *The Invention of Art: A Cultural History* (Chicago: University of Chicago Press, 2001).

4. Eric Moody, "Politics and Museums." In *Museums 2000: Politics, People, Professionals, and Profit.* Edited by Patrick J. Boylan

(London: Routledge, 1992).

5. The relationship between the artist and the market is described by Lee Hye-Kyung in "When Arts Met Marketing," *International Journal of Cultural Policy* 11 (2005): 289-305.

6. Hugh Honour, *Romanticism* (London: Allen Lane, 1979); Larry Shiner, *The Invention of Art: A Cultural History* (Chicago: University of Chicago Press, 2001).

7. On our relationship with museums, see Russell Keat, *Cultural Goods and the Limits of the Market* (London: MacMillan Press, 2000); Linda Moss, "Encouraging Creative Enterprise in Russia." In *Entrepreneurship in the Creative Industries: An International Perspective.* Edited by Colette Henry, (Cheltenham: Edward Elgar, 2007), pp. 142-158; Stephen Weil, *Rethinking the Museum* (Washington: Smithsonian, 1990), p. xviii.

8. Stephen Weil, *Beauty and the Beasts: On Museums, Art, the Law, and the Market* (Washington: Smithsonian, 1983).

9. Ibid.

10. Stephen Weil, *Rethinking the Museum* (Washington: Smithsonian, 1990).

11. Perry T. Rathbone, "Influences of Private Patrons: The Art Museum as an Example." In *The Arts and Public Policy in the United States.* Edited by W. McNeil Lowry (Englewood Cliffs: Prentice-Hall, 1984); Stanley N. Katz, "Influences on Public Policies in the United States." In *The Arts and Public Policy in the United States.* Edited by W. McNeil Lowry (Englewood Cliffs: Prentice-Hall, 1984); W. McNeil Lowry, "Introduction." In *The Arts and Public Policy in the United States.* Edited by W. McNeil Lowry (Englewood Cliffs: Prentice-Hall, 1984); Perry T. Rathbone, "Influences of Private Patrons: The Art Museum as an Example." In *The Arts and Public Policy in the United States.* Edited by W. McNeil Lowry (Englewood Cliffs: Prentice-Hall, 1984); Stephen Weil, *Beauty and the Beasts: On Museums, Art, the Law, and the Market* (Washington: Smithsonian, 1983).

12. John F. Kennedy's quote about the arts is found in "A Symposium: Issues in the Emergence of Public Policy." In *The Arts and Public Policy in the United States.* Edited by W. McNeil Lowry (Englewood Cliffs: Prentice-Hall, 1984).

13. Larry Shiner, *The Invention of Art: A Cultural History* (Chicago: University of Chicago Press, 2001). What is considered high or

low culture changes over time. High culture in one era is pop culture in another. In the 1700s, for example, chamber music was considered pop culture.

14. Stephen Weil, *Beauty and the Beasts: On Museums, Art, the Law, and the Market* (Washington: Smithsonian, 1983).

15. W. McNeil Lowry, "Introduction." In *The Arts and Public Policy in the United States.* Edited by W. McNeil Lowry (Englewood Cliffs: Prentice-Hall, 1984).

16. Stephen Weil, *Beauty and the Beasts: On Museums, Art, the Law, and the Market* (Washington: Smithsonian, 1983); "A Symposium: Issues in the Emergence of Public Policy." In *The Arts and Public Policy in the United States.* Edited by W. McNeil Lowry (Englewood Cliffs: Prentice-Hall, 1984).

17. The definition of the creative industries from The Hong Kong Centre for Cultural Policy Research, University of Hong Kong, is found in "Baseline Study on Hong Kong's Creative Industries," The Government of the Hong Kong Special Administrative Region, September 2003.

18. For more on the creative industries, including their meteoric growth and worth, see *Entrepreneurship in the Creative Industries: An International Perspective.* Edited by Colette Henry (Cheltenham: Edward Elgar, 2007).

19. Colette Henry, "Introduction." In *Entrepreneurship in the Creative Industries: An International Perspective.* Edited by Colette Henry (Cheltenham: Edward Elgar, 2007), pp. 1-6. Note that it's difficult to compare the creative industries from country to country because nations use different definitions and data sources; National Endowment for Science, Technology and the Arts, "Creating Growth: How the UK Can Develop World Class Creative Businesses," April 2006.

20. Calvin Taylor, "Developing Relationships Between Higher Education, Enterprise and Innovation in the Creative Industries." In *Entrepreneurship in the Creative Industries: An International Perspective.* Edited by Colette Henry (Cheltenham: Edward Elgar, 2007), pp. 178-196; Paul J. DiMaggio, "The Nonprofit Instrument and the Influence of the Marketplace on Policies in the Arts." In *The Arts and Public Policy in the United States.* Edited by W. McNeil Lowry (Englewood Cliffs: Prentice-Hall, 1984); "A Symposium: Issues in the Emergence of Public Policy."

In *The Arts and Public Policy in the United States*. Edited by W. McNeil Lowry (Englewood Cliffs: Prentice-Hall, 1984).

21. Ian Youngs, "Radiohead Guitarist Ed O'Brien Warns of Money Pressure," *BBC News*, January 24, 2010.

22. On the rise of the market in the arts, see, for example, Lee Hye-Kyung, "When Arts Met Marketing," *International Journal of Cultural Policy* 11 (2005): 289-305; Paul J. DiMaggio, "The Nonprofit Instrument and the Influence of the Marketplace on Policies in the Arts." In *The Arts and Public Policy in the United States*. Edited by W. McNeil Lowry, (Englewood Cliffs: Prentice-Hall, 1984).

23. Alberta museums, for example, started to see themselves as competing with West Edmonton Mall — then the world's largest mall. See Leslie S. Oakes, Barbara Townley, and David J. Cooper's "Business Planning as Pedagogy: Language and Control in a Changing Institutional Field" *Administrative Science Quarterly* 43 (1998): 257-292.

24. Paul J. DiMaggio, "The Nonprofit Instrument and the Influence of the Marketplace on Policies in the Arts." In *The Arts and Public Policy in the United States*. Edited by W. McNeil Lowry (Englewood Cliffs: Prentice-Hall, 1984).

25. Museum exhibits provided by corporations was reported by Robin Pogrebin in "And Now, An Exhibition From Our Sponsor," *The New York Times* (August 21, 2009).

26. "Swiffer Named 'Official Cleaner of The Children's Museum of Indianapolis,'" Procter & Gamble press release, December 22, 2009, on PR Newswire website; Lee Rosenbaum, blog post on "New Frontiers in Corporate Sponsorship: A Museum's 'Official Cleaner,'" CultureGrrl Blog, posted December 23, 2009.

27. "The Children's Museum of Indianapolis and Mattel Present Barbie™: The Fashion Experience," The Children's Museum of Indianapolis press release, November 13, 2009; Lee Rosenbaum, blog post on "New Frontiers in Corporate Sponsorship: A Museum's 'Official Cleaner,'" CultureGrrl Blog, posted December 23, 2009.

28. Linda Moss, "Encouraging Creative Enterprise in Russia." In *Entrepreneurship in the Creative Industries: An International Perspective*. Edited by Colette Henry (Cheltenham: Edward Elgar, 2007).

29. Quoted in Tom Brown, Stuart Crainer, Des Dearlove and Jorge Nascimento Rodrigues, *Business Minds: Connect with the World's Greatest Management Thinkers* (Prentice Hall Financial Times: London, 2002).

30. See, for example, Maev Kennedy, "Jewellers sponsor Fay Weldon's latest literary gem," *The Guardian*, September 4, 2001.

31. Don Thompson, *The $12 Million Stuffed Shark: The Curious Economics of Contemporary Art* (Toronto: Doubleday Canada, 2008); Adrian Dannatt, "Jeff Koons On His Serpentine Show, His Inspirations and How His Studio System Works," *The Art Newspaper* 204 (2009).

32. Don Thompson, *The $12 Million Stuffed Shark: The Curious Economics of Contemporary Art* (Toronto: Doubleday Canada, 2008).

33. Sean O'Hagan, "Damien of the Dead," *The Observer*, February 19, 2006.

34. Sarah Thornton interviews Takashi Murakami and Marc Jacobs in *Seven Days in the Art World* (New York: W.W. Norton, 2008).

35. Oliver Bennett, *Cultural Policy and the Crisis of Legitimacy: Entrepreneurial Answers in the United Kingdom* (1996) p. 11, Centre for the Study of Cultural Policy, University of Warwick, Coventry, cited in Lee Hye-Kyung, "When Arts Met Marketing," *International Journal of Cultural Policy* 11 (2005): 289-305.

Additional Sources
The first epigraph is from Stanley Kunitz's *The Wild Braid* (New York: W.W. Norton, 2005).
The second epigraph is from economist Tyler Cowen's *In Praise of Commercial Culture* (Cambridge: Harvard University Press, 1998).

9. The Monoculture Effect

1. Richard Feynman tells his story about wobbling plates in Frank Barron, Anthea Barron, and Alfonso Montuori's *Creators on Creating* (New York: Tarcher, 1997).

2. Joseph Campbell talks about following your bliss with Bill Moyers in *The Power of Myth* (New York: Doubleday, 1988).

3. Václav Havel, "The Power of the Powerless." In *Living in Truth*. Edited by Jan Vladislav (London: Faber and Faber, 1989), pp. 36-122.
4. Ibid.
5. Ibid.
6. Craig McInnis and Malcolm Anderson, "Academic work satisfaction in the wake of institutional reforms in Australia." In *The Professoriate*. Edited by Anthony Welch (Dordrecht, Netherlands: Springer, 2005), pp. 133-145.
7. Ibid.
8. Oscar Wilde, *De Profundis, The Ballad of Reading Gaol and Other Writings* (Hertfordshire: Wordsworth Editions, 1999).
9. Abraham Maslow describes higher level human needs and metapathologies in *The Farther Reaches of Human Nature* (New York: Viking, 1971).

Additional Sources
The epigraph is from Karen Armstrong's memoir *The Spiral Staircase* (New York: Alfred A. Knopf, 2004).

10. Finding Another Way

1. Václav Havel, "The Power of the Powerless." In *Living in Truth*, ed. Jan Vladislav (London: Faber and Faber, 1989), pp. 36-122.
2. The criteria for parallel structures are derived from Václav Havel's essay "The Power of the Powerless." In *Living in Truth*. Edited by Jan Vladislav (London: Faber and Faber, 1989), pp. 36-122.
3. Václav Havel, "The Power of the Powerless." In *Living in Truth*. Edited by Jan Vladislav (London: Faber and Faber, 1989), pp. 36-122.
4. E.F. Schumacher, *Small is Beautiful* (New York: Harper & Row, 1973).
5. Wendy Parkins and Geoffrey Craig, *Slow Living* (Oxford: Berg Publishers, 2006).
6. Geoff Andrews, *The Slow Food Story: Politics and Pleasure* (Montreal: McGill-Queen's University Press, 2008).
7. Jean Vanier's comments about the pleasures of eating together are found in *Be Not Afraid* (Toronto: Griffin House, 1975).

8.　Ilse Crawford, *Home is Where the Heart Is* (London: Quadrille, 2005).

9.　Christopher Alexander, *The Timeless Way of Building* (New York: Oxford University Press, 1979).

10.　Ibid.

11.　William Saunders is quoted in a National Building Museum interview with Michael Mehaffy regarding Christopher Alexander and his impact on the profession on the occasion of Alexander being awarded the 2009 Vincent Scully Prize.

12.　Christopher Alexander, "The Origins of Pattern Theory, the Future of the Theory, and the Generation of a Living World." Keynote speech delivered at the ACM Conference on Object-Oriented Programs, Systems, Languages and Applications, 1996.

13.　Christopher Alexander, *The Timeless Way of Building* (New York: Oxford University Press, 1979).

14.　Ibid.

15.　For a detailed explanation of the four components of the Nonviolent Communication method, what a conversation using the method sounds like in practice, and how to use the method in your own life, see Dr. Marshall Rosenberg's *Nonviolent Communication: A Language of Life* (Encinitas, California: PuddleDancer Press, 2003) or visit www.CNVC.org and www.NonviolentCommunication.com.

16.　Marshall Rosenberg, *Nonviolent Communication: A Language of Life* (Encinitas, California: PuddleDancer Press, 2003).

17.　Ibid. See also, www.NonviolentCommunication.com.

18.　Albert Einstein, *Ideas and Opinions* (New York: Wings, 1954).

Additional Sources

The epigraph is from Erich Fromm's *To Have or To Be?* (New York: Harper & Row, 1976).

Epilogue

The first epigraph is from Leo Tolstoy's *War and Peace* trans. Richard Pevear and Larissa Volokhonsky (New York: Knopf, 2007).

The second epigraph is from Clarissa Pinkola Estés *Women Who Run With the Wolves* (New York: Random House, 1992).

BIBLIOGRAPHY

"A Symposium: Issues in the Emergence of Public Policy." In *The Arts and Public Policy in the United States*. Edited by W. McNeil Lowry Englewood Cliffs: Prentice-Hall, 1984.

Adams, John. *Political Writings of John Adams*. Edited by George W. Carey Washington, DC: Regnery Publishing, 2000.

Alexander, Christopher, Sara Ishikawa, Murray Silverstein, Max Jacobxon, Ingrid Fiksdahl-King, and Shlomo Angel. *A Pattern Language*. New York: Oxford University Press, 1977.

Alexander, Christopher. *The Timeless Way of Building*. New York: Oxford University Press, 1979.

Alford, C. Fred. "Whistle-blowers," *American Behavioral Scientist* 43 (1999): 264-277.

Alire, Camila. "The Library Professional." In *Perspectives, Insights & Priorities: 17 Leaders Speak Freely of Librarianship*. Edited by Norman Horrocks Lanham, MD: Scarecrow Press, 2005.

American Library Association, *The Freedom to Read Statement*. Office of Intellectual Freedom. Adopted June 25, 1953.

American Medical Association, *Opinions and Reports of the Judicial Council*, 1966.

Amos, Jonathan. "Study Limits Maximum Tree Height." *BBC News*, April 21, 2004.

Andrews, Geoff. *The Slow Food Story: Politics and Pleasure.* Montreal: McGill-Queen's University Press, 2008.

Ariely, Dan. *Predictably Irrational.* New York: HarperCollins, 2008.

Armstrong, Karen. *The Spiral Staircase.* New York: Knopf, 2004.

"Arts Degrees 'Reduce Earnings.'" *BBC News,* March 6, 2003.

Asimov, Isaac. *I. Asimov, a Memoir.* New York: Doubleday, 1994.

Austin, James and Garry Coventry. *Emerging Issues on Privatized Prisons.* San Francisco, CA: National Council on Crime and Delinquency, 2001.

Bailyn, Lotte, Robert Drago, and Thomas A. Kochan. *Integrating Work and Family Life: A Holistic Approach.* Sloan Work-Family Policy Network, September 14, 2001.

Barron, Frank, Anthea Barron, and Alfonso Montuori. *Creators on Creating.* New York: Tarcher, 1997.

Basken, Paul. "Medical Journals See a Cost to Fighting Industry-Backed Research." *Chronicle of Higher Education,* September 13, 2009.

Bauman, Zygmunt. *Society Under Siege.* Cambridge, UK: Polity Press, 2002.

Becker, Brian and Barry Gerhart. "The Impact of Human Resource Management on Organizational Performance: Progress and Prospects." *Academy of Management Journal* 39(1996): 779-801

Bennett, Oliver. *Cultural Policy and the Crisis of Legitimacy: Entrepreneurial Answers in the United Kingdom.* Centre for the Study of Cultural Policy. Coventry: University of Warwick, 1996.

Berry III, John N. "Election 2004: The Library Fails Again." In *Perspectives, Insights & Priorities: 17 Leaders Speak Freely of Librarianship.* Edited by Norman Horrocks Lanham, MD: Scarecrow Press, 2005.

Bianchi, Suzanne M., John P. Robinson, and Melissa A. Milkie. *Changing Rhythms in American Family Life.* New York: Russell Sage, 2007.

Blumenthal, David, Eric G. Campbell, NancyAnne Causino, and Karen Seashore Louis. "Participation of Life-Science Faculty in Research Relationships with Industry." *New England Journal of Medicine* 335(1996): 1734-1739.

Borins, Sandford. "New Public Management, North American Style," In *New Public Management: Current Trends and Future Prospects.* Edited by Kate McLaughlin, Stephen P. Osborne, and Ewan Ferlie London: Routledge, 2002, pp. 181-194.

Bousquet, Marc. *How the University Works: Higher Education and the Low-Wage Nation*. New York: New York University Press, 2008.

Bowe, John, Marisa Bowe, and Sabin Streeter. *Gig: Americans Talk About Their Jobs at the Turn of the Millennium* (New York: Crown, 2000).

Brisbois, Richard. *How Canada Stacks Up: The Quality of Work – An International Perspective*. Canadian Policy Research Networks, December 19, 2003.

Breneman, David W., Brian Pusser, and Sarah E. Turner. "The Contemporary Provision of For-Profit Higher Education." In *Earnings From Learning*. Edited by David W. Breneman, Brian Pusser, and Sarah E. Turner New York: State University of New York Press, 2006.

Broadbent, Jane and Richard Laughlin. "Public Service Professionals and the New Public Management: Control of the Professions in the Public Services." In *New Public Management: Current Trends and Future Prospects*. Edited by Kate McLaughlin, Stephen P. Osborne, and Ewan Ferlie London: Routledge, 2002.

Brown, Tom, Stuart Crainer, Des Dearlove and Jorge Nascimento Rodrigues. *Business Minds: Connect with the World's Greatest Management Thinkers*. Prentice Hall Financial Times: London, 2002.

Budde, Michael L. "Collecting Praise: Global Culture Industries." In *The Blackwell Companion to Christian Ethics*. Edited by Stanley Hauerwas and Samuel Wells Malden, MA: Blackwell, 2004.

Budde, Michael and Robert Brimlow. *Christianity Incorporated*. Grand Rapids, MI: Brazos Press, 2002.

Bunting, Madeleine. *Willing Slaves: How the Overwork Culture is Ruling Our Lives*. Toronto: HarperCollins, 2004.

Butler Bass, Diana. *A People's History of Christianity*. New York: HarperOne, 2007.

Campbell, Evelyn M., Suzanne Duncan, Sonal Rastogi, and Joan Wilson. "The Future is Now: Will Public Libraries Survive?" In *Reinvention of the Public Library for the 21st Century*. Edited by William L. Whitesides Sr., Englewood, CO: Libraries Unlimited, 1998.

Caldwell, Kirbyjon and Walt Kallestad. *Entrepreneurial Faith*. Colorado Springs: Waterbrook Press, 2004.

Callahan, Daniel. *False Hopes: Why America's Quest For Perfect Health is a Recipe for Failure*. New York: Simon & Schuster, 1998.

Campbell, Eric G., Joshua B. Powers, David Blumenthal, and Brian Biles. "Inside the Triple Helix: Technology Transfer and Commercialization in the Life Sciences." *Health Affairs* 23(2004): 64-76.

Campbell, Joseph, with Bill Moyers. *The Power of Myth*. New York: Doubleday, 1988.

Canadian Millennium Scholarship Foundation. Brief Submitted to The House of Commons Standing Committee on Finance 2006 Pre-Budget Consultations.

Cappelli, Peter. *The New Deal at Work: Managing the Market-Driven Workforce*. Boston: Harvard Business School Press, 1999.

Caputo, Ibby. "Probing Doctors' Ties to Industry." *The Washington Post*, August 18, 2009.

Catford, John. "Social Entrepreneurs are Vital for Health Promotion – but They Need Supportive Environments Too." *Health Promotion International* 13(1998): 95-97.

Central Policy Unit. *Baseline Study on Hong Kong's Creative Industries*. Government of the Hong Kong Special Administrative Region, September 2003.

Children's Museum of Indianapolis. *The Children's Museum of Indianapolis and Mattel Present Barbie™: The Fashion Experience*. Press Release. November 13, 2009.

Cobb Jr., John B. *Sustaining the Common Good*. Cleveland: Pilgrim Press, 1994.

Coffman, Steve. "What If You Ran Your Library Like a Bookstore?" *American Libraries* 29(1998): 40-46.

Conn, Peter. "We Need to Acknowledge the Realities of Employment in the Humanities." *The Chronicle Review*, April 4, 2010.

Connelly, Catherine E. and Daniel G. Gallagher. "Emerging Trends in Contingent Work Research." *Journal of Management* 30(2004): 959-983.

Cowen, Tyler. *In Praise of Commercial Culture*. Cambridge: Harvard University Press, 1998.

Crawford, Ilse. *Home is Where the Heart Is*. London: Quadrille, 2005.

D'Angelo, Ed. *Barbarians at the Gates of the Public Library*. Duluth, MN: Library Juice Press, 2006.

Daily, Gretchen C. *Nature's Services: Societal Dependence on Natural Ecosystems*. Washington, DC: Island Press, 1997.

Dane, Perry. "The Corporation Sole and the Encounter of Law and Church." In *Sacred Companies*. Edited by N. J. Demerath III, Peter Dobkin Hall, Terry Schmitt, and Rhys H. Williams Oxford, Oxford University Press: 1998.

Dannatt, Adrian. "Jeff Koons On His Serpentine Show, His Inspirations and How His Studio System Works." *The Art Newspaper* 204(2009).

Dawson, Sandra and Charlotte Dargie. "New Public Management: A Discussion with Special Reference to UK Health." In *New Public Management: Current Trends and Future Prospects*. Edited by Kate McLaughlin, Stephen P. Osborne, and Ewan Ferlie London: Routledge, 2002.

Dees, J. Gregory, Jed Emerson and Peter Economy. *Enterprising Nonprofits: A Toolkit for Social Entrepreneurs*. New York: Wiley, 2001.

Dees, Gregory. "Enterprising Nonprofits." *Harvard Business Review*, January(1998): 54-67.

De George, Richard. *Business Ethics: Fourth Edition*. New Jersey: Prentice Hall, 1995.

Dembicki, Geoff. "Librarians Told to Stand on Guard for 2010 Sponsors." *The Tyee*, January 12, 2010.

Deutsch, Francine M. *Halving It All: How Equally Shared Parenting Works*. Cambridge, MA: Harvard University Press. Cited in Lotte Bailyn, Robert Drago, and Thomas A. Kochan, *Integrating Work and Family Life: A Holistic Approach*. Sloan Work-Family Policy Network, September 14, 2001.

DiMaggio, Paul J. "The Nonprofit Instrument and the Influence of the Marketplace on Policies in the Arts." In *The Arts and Public Policy in the United States*. Edited by W. McNeil Lowry Englewood Cliffs: Prentice-Hall, 1984.

Drucker, Peter F. *The Practice of Management*. New York: HarperBusiness, 1954.

Duxbury, Linda and Chris Higgins. *Work-Life Balance in the New Millennium*. Canadian Policy Research Networks, October 23, 2001.

Edington, Dee W. "Emerging Research: A View From One Research Center." *American Journal of Health Promotion* 15(2001): 341-349.

Eikenberry, Angela M., and Jodie Drapal Kluver. "The Marketization of the Nonprofit Sector: Civil Society at Risk?" *Public Administration Review* 64(2004): 132-140.

Einstein, Albert. *Ideas and Opinions*. New York: Wings Books, 1954.

Engell, James and Anthony Dangerfield. "The Market-Model University: Humanities in the Age of Money." *Harvard Alumni Magazine*, May/June(1998).

Estabrook, Leigh S. "A Virtuous Profession." In *Perspectives, Insights & Priorities: 17 Leaders Speak Freely of Librarianship*. Edited by Norman Horrocks Lanham, MD: Scarecrow Press, 2005.

Estés, Clarissa Pinkola. *Women Who Run With the Wolves*. New York: Random House, 1992.

Feinstein, David, and Stanley Krippner, *The Mythic Path*. New York: Putnam Books, 1997.

Frenette, Marc. "The Impact of Tuition Fees on University Access: Evidence From a Large-Scale Price Deregulation in Professional Programs." *Statistics Canada* 11F0019MIE - Number 263(2005).

Finke, Roger, Avery M. Guest, and Rodney Stark. "Mobilizing local religious markets: Religious pluralism in the empire state, 1855-1865." *American Sociological Review* 61(1996): 203-218.

Folbre, Nancy. *The Invisible Heart: Economics and Family Values*. New York: New Press, 2001.

Fowler, James W. *Stages of Faith: The Psychology of Human Development and the Quest for Meaning*. New York: HarperCollins, 1995.

Freidson, Eliot. *Medical Work in America: Essays on Health Care*. New Haven: Yale University Press, 1989.

Friedman, David D. *Law's Order: What Economics Has to do With Law and Why It Matters*. Princeton, NJ: Princeton University Press, 2000.

Friedman, Thomas L. *The Lexus and the Olive Tree: Understanding Globalization*. New York: Farrar Straus Giroux, 1999.

Fromm, Erich. *To Have or To Be?* New York: Harper & Row, 1976.

Fulford, Robert. *The Triumph of Narrative*. New York: Broadway, 2000.

Galbraith, John Kenneth. *Economics in Perspective: A Critical History*. Boston: Houghton Mifflin, 1987.

Galilei, Galileo. *Dialogue on the Great World Systems, The Salisbury Translation*. Edited by G. de Santillana Chicago: University of Chicago Press, 1953.

Garceau, Oliver. *The Public Library in the Political Process*. New York: Columbia University Press, 1949.

Geertz, Clifford. *Available Light*. Princeton, NJ: Princeton University Press, 2000.

Gelade, Garry A. and Mark Ivery. "The Impact of Human Resource Management and Work Climate on Organizational Performance." *Personnel Psychology* 56(2003): 383-405.

Goldin, Claudia. *Understanding the Gender Gap: An Economic History of American Women*. New York: Oxford University Press, 1990.

Gorman, Michael. "Library Values in a Changing World." In *Perspectives, Insights & Priorities: 17 Leaders Speak Freely of Librarianship*. Edited by Norman Horrocks Lanham, MD: Scarecrow Press, 2005.

Gose, Ben. "A Revolution was Ventured, But What Did It Gain?" *Chronicle of Philanthropy* 15(2003): 6-9.

Gopalkrishnan, Iyer. "International Exchanges as the Basis for Conceptualizing Ethics in International Business." *Journal of Business Ethics* 31(2001): 3-24.

Graham, Billy. *Billy Graham, God's Ambassador*. New York: HarperOne, 2007.

Gray, B. H. and W. J. McNerney. "For-profit Enterprise in Health Care: The Institute of Medicine Study." *New England Journal of Medicine* 314(1986): 1523-1528.

Green, Gareth M. and Frank Baker. *Work, Health and Productivity*. Oxford: Oxford University Press, 1991.

Grove, Andrew. *High Output Management*. New York: Vintage, 1995.

Guder, Darrell. *The Continuing Conversion of the Church*. Grand Rapids, MI: William B. Eerdmans, 2000.

Hammond, Jason. "Cash Cow: User Fees in Alberta Public Libraries." *Partnership: the Canadian Journal of Library and Information Practice and Research* 2(2007).

Hari, Johann. "Johann Hari: And now for some good news." *The Independent*, August 6, 2010.

Havel, Václav. "The Power of the Powerless." In *Living in Truth*. Edited by Jan Vladislav London: Faber and Faber, 1989.

Haycock, Ken. "Librarianship: Intersecting Perspectives for the Academy and From the Field." In *Perspectives, Insights & Priorities: 17 Leaders Speak Freely of Librarianship.* Edited by Norman Horrocks Lanham, MD: Scarecrow Press, 2005.

Henry, Colette. *Entrepreneurship in the Creative Industries: An International Perspective.* Edited by Colette Henry, Cheltenham: Edward Elgar, 2007.

Herzlinger, Regina. *Who Killed Health Care? America's $2 Trillion Dollar Medical Problem—And the Consumer-Driven Cure.* New York: McGraw-Hill, 2007.

Hewlett, Sylvia Ann. "Executive Women and the Myth of Having It All." *Harvard Business Review* 80(2002): 66.

Hibbert, Kathryn and Luigi Iannacci. "From Dissemination to Discernment: The Commodification of Literacy Instruction and the Fostering of Good Teacher Consumerism." *Reading Teacher* 58(2005): 716-727.

Himmelstein, David U., Deborah Thorne, Elizabeth Warren, and Steffie Woolhandler. "Medical Bankruptcy in the United States, 2007: Results of a National Study." *American Journal of Medicine* 122(2009): 741-746.

Hochschild, Arlie Russell. *The Time Bind: When Work Becomes Home and Home Becomes Work.* New York: Metropolitan Books, 1997.

Holland, Kelley. "Working Long Hours, and Paying a Price." *The New York Times*, July 27, 2008.

Honour, Hugh. *Romanticism.* London: Allen Lane, 1979.

Hye-Kyung, Lee. "When Arts Met Marketing." *International Journal of Cultural Policy* 11(2005): 289-305.

"Jesus, CEO; Churches as Businesses." *The Economist* 377(2005): 41-44.

Johannesson, Ingolfur Asgeir, Sverker Lindblad, and Hannu Simola. "An Inevitable Progress? Educational Restructuring in Finland, Iceland, and Sweden at the Turn of the Millennium." *Scandinavian Journal of Educational Research* 46(2002): 325-339.

Junor, Sean and Alex Usher. "The End of Need-Based Student Financial Aid in Canada?" *Educational Policy Institute*, 2007.

Kalleberg, Arne L. "Nonstandard Employment Relations: Part-time, Temporary and Contract Work." *Annual Review of Sociology* 26(2000): 341-365.

Katz, Stanley N. "Influences on Public Policies in the United States." In *The Arts and Public Policy in the United States*. Edited by W. McNeil Lowry Englewood Cliffs: Prentice-Hall, 1984.

Keat, Russell. *Cultural Goods and the Limits of the Market*. London: MacMillan Press, 2000.

Kennedy, Maev. "Jewellers sponsor Fay Weldon's latest literary gem." *The Guardian*, September 4, 2001.

Kenneson, Philip and James Street. *Selling Out the Church*. Eugene, Oregon: Wipf & Stock, 2003.

Kok, Peter, Ton van der Wiele, Richard McKenna, and Alan A. Brown. "A Corporate Social Responsibility Audit within a Quality Management Framework." *Journal of Business Ethics* 31(2001): 285-297.

Krebs, Angelika. *Ethics of Nature*. Berlin: Walter de Gruyter, 1999.

Knijn, Trudie. "Marketization and the Struggling Logics of (Home) Care in the Netherlands." In *Care Work: Gender, Class, and the Welfare State*. Edited by Madonna Harrington Meyer New York: Routledge, 2000.

Kunitz, Stanley. *The Wild Braid*. New York: W.W. Norton, 2005.

Lane, Megan. "Is This the Library of the Future?" *BBC News*, March 18, 2003.

Lonne, Bob, Catherine McDonald and Tricia Fox. "Ethical Practice in the Contemporary Human Services." *Journal of Social Work* 4(2004): 345-367.

Lowry, W. McNeil. "Introduction." In *The Arts and Public Policy in the United States*. Edited by W. McNeil Lowry, Englewood Cliffs: Prentice-Hall, 1984.

Lynn Jr., Laurence E. *Public Management: Old and New*. New York: Routledge, 2006.

National Geographic. "Ecosystem Investments Could Yield Trillions of Dollars in Benefits, Study Finds." *NATGEO Newswatch*, November 13, 2009.

———. *Our Relationship With Nature, A Fragile System Sustains Us: Nature Reveals Its True Value*. http://www.nationalgeographic. com/earthpulse/ecosystem-and-conservation.html.

Macfarlane, Bruce and Ming Cheng. "Communism, Universalism and Disinterestedness: Re-examining Contemporary Support Among Academics for Merton's Scientific Norms." *Journal of Academic Ethics* 6(2008): 67-78.

Mair, Johanna and Ignasi Marti. "Social Entrepreneurship Research: A Source of Explanation, Prediction, and Delight." *Journal of World Business* 41(2006): 36-44.

Mardiros, Shelley. "Banff's Very Public Library." *AlbertaViews* 4(2001): 37-39.

Marginson, Simon. "National and Global Competition in Higher Education." *Australian Educational Researcher* 31(2004): 1-28.

Marglin, Stephen. *The Dismal Science: How Thinking Like An Economist Undermines Community.* Cambridge: Harvard University Press, 2008.

Maslow, Abraham. *The Farther Reaches of Human Nature.* New York: Viking, 1971.

McCabe, Ronald. *Civic Librarianship: Renewing the Social Mission of the Public Library.* Lanham, MD: Scarecrow Press, 2001.

McInnis, Craig and Malcolm Anderson. "Academic work satisfaction in the wake of institutional reforms in Australia." In *The Professoriate.* Edited by Anthony Welch Dordrecht, Netherlands: Springer, 2005.

Mok, Ka-ho. "Education and the Market Place in Hong Kong and Mainland China." *Higher Education* 37(1999): 133-158.

———. "The Cost of Managerialism: The Implications for the 'McDonaldisation' of Higher Education in Hong Kong." *Journal of Higher Education Policy* 21(1999): 117-127.

Moody, Eric. "Politics and Museums." In *Museums 2000: Politics, People, Professionals, and Profit.* Edited by Patrick J. Boylan London: Routledge, 1992.

Mooney, Harold A. and Paul R. Ehrlich. "Ecosystem Services: A Fragmentary History." In *Nature's Services: Societal Dependence on Natural Ecosystems.* Edited by Gretchen C. Daily Washington, DC: Island Press (1997): 11-19.

Morris, Norval. "The Contemporary Prison: 1965-Present." In *The Oxford History of the Prison: The Practice of Punishment in Western Society.* Edited by Norval Morris and David J. Rothman New York: Oxford University Press, 1995.

Morris, Norval and David J. Rothman. "Introduction." In *The Oxford History of the Prison: The Practice of Punishment in Western Society.* Edited by Norval Morris and David J. Rothman New York: Oxford University Press, 1995.

Moss, Linda. "Encouraging Creative Enterprise in Russia." In *Entrepreneurship in the Creative Industries: An International Perspective*. Edited by Colette Henry Cheltenham: Edward Elgar, 2007.

Mother Teresa. *No Greater Love*. New York: New World Library, 2002.

Mursell, John. *Principles of Democratic Education*. New York: W.W. Norton, 1955.

National Endowment for Science, Technology and the Arts. *Creating Growth: How the UK Can Develop World Class Creative Businesses*. April, 2006.

Oakes, Leslie S., Barbara Townley, and David J. Cooper. "Business Planning as Pedagogy: Language and Control in a Changing Institutional Field." *Administrative Science Quarterly* 43(1998): 257-292.

Oder, Norman. "When LSSI Comes to Town." *Library Journal*, October 1, 2004.

O'Hagan, Sean. "Damien of the Dead." *The Observer*, February 19, 2006.

Okri, Ben. *A Way of Being Free*. London: Phoenix House, 1997.

Oplatka, Izhar, Jane Hesley-Brown, and Nick H. Foskett. "The Voice of Teachers in Marketing Their School." *School Leadership & Management* 22(2002): 177-196.

Osborne, Stephen P. and Kate McLaughlin. "The New Public Management in Context." In *New Public Management: Current Trends and Future Prospects*. Edited by Kate McLaughlin, Stephen P. Osborne, and Ewan Ferlie London: Routledge, 2002.

Osterman, Paul. "Work/Family Programs and the Employment Relationship." *Administrative Science Quarterly* 40(1995): 681-700.

"'Overwork' kills Toyota employee." *BBC News*, July 10, 2008.

Pappenheim, Fritz. "Alienation in American Society." *Monthly Review* June(2000).

Parkins, Wendy and Geoffrey Craig. *Slow Living*. Oxford: Berg, 2006.

Paul, Pamela. "Childless by Choice." *American Demographics* 23(2001): 44-50.

Pearce, Michael. "The Marketization of Discourse About Education in UK General Election Manifestos." *Text* 24(2004): 245-265.

Peredo, Ana Maria. "Nothing thicker than blood? Commentary on 'Help one another, use one another: Toward an anthropology of family business.'" *Entrepreneurship Theory & Practice* 27(2003): 397-400.

Perrow, Charles. *Organizing America: Wealth, Power, and the Origins of Corporate Capitalism*. Princeton, NJ: Princeton University Press, 2002.

Peters, Tom. "The Brand Called You." *Fast Company* 10(1997): 83.

Pew Forum on Religion and Public Life. *U.S. Religious Landscape Survey*, 2007.

Pink, Daniel. "Free Agent Nation." *Fast Company* 12(December 1997).

Pipher, Mary. "In Praise of Hometowns." In *Sustainable Planet: Solutions for the Twenty-First Century*. Edited by Juliet B. Schor and Betsy Taylor Boston: Beacon Press, 2002.

Pogrebin, Robin. "And Now, An Exhibition From Our Sponsor." *The New York Times*, August 21, 2009.

Polivka, Anne E. and Thomas Nardone. "On the Definition of 'Contingent Work.'" *Monthly Labor Review* 112(1989): 9-16.

Porter, Michael E. and Elizabeth Olmsted Teisberg. *Redefining Health Care: Creating Value-Based Competition on Results*. Cambridge: Harvard Business School Press, 2006.

Power, Sally and Geoff Whitty. "Teaching New Subjects? The Hidden Curriculum of Marketized Education Systems." Paper presented at the annual meeting of the American Educational Research Association, Chicago, Illinois, March 24-28, 1997.

Powers, Joshua B. "Patents and Royalties." In *Privatization and Public Universities*. Edited by Douglas M. Priest and Edward P. St. John Bloomington: Indiana University Press, 2006.

Pratchett, Lawrence and Melvin Wingfield. "Petty bureaucracy and Woolly-minded Liberalism? The Changing Ethos of Local Government Officers." *Public Adminstration* 74(1996): 639-656.

Press, Eyal and Jennifer Washburn. "The Kept University." *The Atlantic Monthly* 285(2000): 39-53.

Priest, Douglas M., and Rachel Dykstra Boon. "Incentive-based Budgeting Systems in the Emerging Environment." In *Earnings From Learning*. Edited by David W. Breneman, Brian Pusser, and Sarah E. Turner New York: State University of New York Press, 2006.

Priest, Douglas M. and Edward P. St. John. *Privatization and Public Universities*. Bloomington: Indiana University Press, 2006.

Procter & Gamble. "Swiffer Named 'Official Cleaner of The Children's Museum of Indianapolis.'" Press Release. December 22, 2009.

"Product Placement in the Pews? Microtargeting meets Megachurches." Knowledge@Wharton, November 15, 2006.

Pruzan, Peter. "The Question of Organizational Consciousness: Can Organizations Have Values, Virtues and Visions?" *Journal of Business Ethics* 29(2001): 271-284.

Pusser, Brian. "Higher Education, Markets, and the Preservation of the Public Good." In *Earnings From Learning*. Edited by David W. Breneman, Brian Pusser, and Sarah E. Turner New York: State University of New York Press, 2006.

"Q&A with Gretchen Daily, Woods Institute Fellow and Professor of Biological Sciences." *Stanford Report*, August 2, 2007.

Qiping, Yin. "The 'Marketisation' of Chinese Higher Education: A Critical Assessment." *Comparative Education*, 30(1994): 217-233.

Raphael, Molly. "Why Do Libraries Matter in the 21st Century?" In *Perspectives, Insights & Priorities: 17 Leaders Speak Freely of Librarianship*. Edited by Norman Horrocks Lanham, MD: Scarecrow Press, 2005.

Rathbone, Perry T. "Influences of Private Patrons: The Art Museum as an Example." In *The Arts and Public Policy in the United States*. Edited by W. McNeil Lowry Englewood Cliffs: Prentice-Hall, 1984.

Ravetz, Jerome R. *Scientific Knowledge and its Social Problems*. New York: Oxford University Press, 1971.

Reamer, F.G. *Ethical Standards in Social Work: A Critical Review of the NASW Code of Ethics*. Washington: NASW Press, 1983.

Regan, Kelly. "Fossil Fuels Official Gives Oil, Gas Support." *Charleston Gazette*, January 31, 2002.

Reis, Thomas and Stephanie Clohesy. *Unleashing New Resources and Entrepreneurship for the Common Good*. Battle Creek, MI: Kellogg Foundation, 1999.

Relman, Arnold S. *A Second Opinion*. New York: Public Affairs, 2007.

Rhode, Deborah L. *In the Interests of Justice: Reforming the Legal Profession*. New York: Oxford University Press, 2000.

Riddell, Sheila and Alastair Wilson. "Captured Customers: People with Learning Difficulties in the Social Market." *British Educational Research Journal* 25(1999): 445-461.

Rikowski, Ruth. "The Corporate Takeover of Libraries" *Information for Social Change* 14(2002).

Rizvi, Fazal. "The Ideology of Privatization in Higher Education: A Global Perspective." In *Earnings From Learning*. Edited by David W. Breneman, Brian Pusser, and Sarah E. Turner New York: State University of New York Press, 2006.

Roberts, Peter. "The Future of the University: Reflections from New Zealand." *International Review of Education* 45(1999): 65-86.

Rosenbaum, Lee. "New Frontiers in Corporate Sponsorship: A Museum's 'Official Cleaner.'" *CultureGrrl Blog*, December 23, 2009.

Rosenberg, Marshall B. *Nonviolent Communication: A Language of Life*. Encinitas, CA: PuddleDancer Press, 2003.

Rothman, David J. "Perfecting the Prison: United States, 1789-1865." In *The Oxford History of the Prison: The Practice of Punishment in Western Society*. Edited by Norval Morris and David J. Rothman New York: Oxford University Press, 1995.

Rowley, Tim, and Shawn Berman. "A Brand New Brand of Corporate Social Performance." *Business and Society* 39(2000): 397-418.

Sagoff, Mark. *The Economy of the Earth*. New York: Cambridge University Press, 2008.

Sapp, John R. *Making Partner: A Guide for Law Firm Associates, Third Edition*. U.S.: American Bar Association Law Practice Management Section, 2006.

Schmidt, Steve. "Prison Guards Lock Up Bundle in OT Pay." *San Diego Union Tribune*, February 28, 2006.

Shichor, David. *Punishment for Profit*. Thousand Oaks, CA: Sage, 1995.

Schiller, Herbert I. *Culture, Inc*. Oxford: Oxford University Press, 1989.

Schumacher, E.F. *Small is Beautiful: Economics as if People Mattered*. New York: Harper & Row, 1973.

Scitovsky, Tibor. *The Joyless Economy*. New York: Oxford University Press, 1992.

Shell Report 1998, *Profits and Principles—does there have to be a choice?* http://ow.ly/4fUPn.

Shiner, Larry. *The Invention of Art: A Cultural History*. Chicago: University of Chicago Press, 2001.

Slaughter, Sheila and Larry Leslie. *Academic Capitalism: Politics, Policies, and the Entrepreneurial University*. Baltimore: Johns Hopkins University Press, 1997.

Slaughter, Sheila and Gary Rhoades. *Academic Capitalism and the New Economy*. Baltimore: Johns Hopkins University Press, 2004.

Solomon, Robert. *Love: Emotion, Myth and Metaphor*. New York: Doubleday, 1981.

St. John, Edward P., and Ontario S. Wooden, "Privatization and Federal Funding for Higher Education." In *Privatization and Public Universities*. Edited by Douglas M. Priest and Edward P. St. John Bloomington: Indiana University Press, 2006.

Stark, Rodney, Roger Finke, and Laurence Iannaccone. "Pluralism and Piety: England and Wales, 1851." *Journal for the Scientific Study of Religion* 34(1995): 431-444.

Starr, Paul. *The Social Transformation of American Medicine*. New York: Basic Books, 1982.

Stevens, Rosemary. *American Medicine and the Public Interest*. New Haven: Yale University Press, 1971.

———. *In Sickness and in Wealth: American Hospitals in the Twentieth Century*. Baltimore: Johns Hopkins University Press, 1999.

Stoline, Anne and Jonathan P. Weiner. *The New Medical Marketplace: A Physician's Guide to the Health Care Revolution*. Baltimore: Johns Hopkins University Press, 1988.

Stormer, Flora. "Making the Shift: Moving From 'Ethics Pays' to an Inter-Systems Model of Business." *Journal of Business Ethics* 44(2003): 279-289.

———. "The Logic of Contingent Work and Overwork." *Relations Industrielles/Industrial Relations* 63(2008): 343-362.

Streitfeld, David. "Anger as a Private Company takes Over Libraries." *The New York Times*, September 26, 2010.

Symons, Ann K. "The More Things Change, the More Things Remain the Same." In *Perspectives, Insights & Priorities: 17 Leaders Speak Freely of Librarianship*. Edited by Norman Horrocks Lanham, MD: Scarecrow Press, 2005.

Tan, Jason. "The Marketisation of Education in Singapore: Policies and Implications." *International Review of Education* 44(1998): 47-63.

Taylor, Calvin. "Developing Relationships Between Higher Education, Enterprise and Innovation in the Creative Industries." In *Entrepreneurship in the Creative Industries: An International Perspective*. Edited by Colette Henry Cheltenham: Edward Elgar, 2007.

Taylor, Charles. *The Malaise of Modernity*. Toronto: Anansi Press, 1991.

Terkel, Studs. *Coming of Age*. New York: New Press, 1995.

Thompson, Don. *The $12 Million Stuffed Shark: The Curious Economics of Contemporary Art*. Toronto: Doubleday Canada, 2008.

Thornton, Sarah. *Seven Days in the Art World*. New York: W.W. Norton, 2008.

Tolstoy, Leo. *War and Peace*. Translated by Richard Pevear and Larissa Volokhonsky New York: Alfred A. Knopf, 2007.

Trosow, Samuel E. and Kirsti Nilsen. *Constraining Public Libraries: The World Trade Organization's General Agreement on Trade in Services*. Lanham, MD: Scarecrow Press, 2006.

U.S. Bureau of the Census. *Statistical Abstract of the U.S.* Washington, D.C., 2002.

U.S. Bureau of Labor Statistics. *Issues in Labor Statistics: Twenty-First Century Moonlighters*, U.S. Department of Labor, September 2002.

Vanier, Jean. *Be Not Afraid*. Toronto: Griffin House, 1975.

Watson, Robert N. "The Humanities Really Do Produce a Profit." *Chronicle of Higher Education*, March 21, 2010.

Weber, Max. *The Protestant Ethic and the Spirit of Capitalism*. New York: Scribner, 1976.

Weil, Stephen. *Beauty and the Beasts: On Museums, Art, the Law, and the Market*. Washington, D.C.: Smithsonian, 1983.

———. *Rethinking the Museum*. Washington, D.C.: Smithsonian, 1990.

Wilde, Oscar. *De Profundis, The Ballad of Reading Gaol and Other Writings*. Hertfordshire: Wordsworth Editions, 1999.

Wilson, Duff and Natasha Singer. "Ghostwriting is Called Rife in Medical Journals." *The New York Times*, September 11, 2009.

Winson, Anthony, and Belinda Leach. *Contingent Work, Disrupted Lives: Labour and Community in the New Rural Economy*. Toronto: University of Toronto Press, 2002.

Wolfe, Alan. *Whose Keeper? Social Science and Moral Obligation.*
   Berkeley: University of California Press, 1989.

World Business Council for Sustainable Development. *Mobility for
   Development: Facts and Trends.* September, 2007.

Wright, Susan. "Markets, Corporations, Consumers? New
   Landscapes of Higher Education." *Learning & Teaching in the
   Social Sciences* 1(2004): 71-93.

Youngs, Ian. "Radiohead Guitarist Ed O'Brien Warns of Money
   Pressure." *BBC News,* January 24, 2010.

INDEX

ABOUT THE AUTHOR

TO LEARN MORE ABOUT the research behind this book, and to share your own stories about the monoculture and parallel structures, please visit *fsmichaels.com*. F.S. Michaels describes herself as "a deep generalist" — someone who looks for unexpected patterns and connections across a broad range of cultural systems, organizations, and human interactions. Her research and writing have been supported by the Social Sciences and Humanities Research Council of Canada, the Killam Trusts, and regional and municipal arts councils. Michaels has an MBA, and lives and writes in British Columbia.

CPSIA information can be obtained at www.ICGtesting.com
Printed in the USA
BVOW04s1543150214

344990BV00002B/19/P